Beyond
the Siege of
Leningrad

Beyond
the Siege of
Leningrad

One Woman's Life during
and after the Occupation

The recollections of
Evdokiia Vasil'evna Baskakova-Bogacheva

Edited by
Oleg Beyda and **Pavel Gavrilov**

CEU PRESS

Central European University Press
Budapest—Vienna—New York

Published in 2024 by
Central European University Press
Nádor utca 11, H-1051 Budapest, Hungary
Tel: +36-1-327-3138 or 327-3000
E-mail: ceupress@press.ceu.edu
Website: www.ceupress.com

ISBN 978-963-386-712-9 (hardback)
ISBN 978-963-386-763-1 (paperback)
ISBN 978-963-386-713-6 (ebook)

Library of Congress Cataloging-in-Publication Data

Names: Baskakova-Bogacheva, Evdokiia Vasil'evna, 1888-1976, author. |
   Beyda, Oleg, editor. | Gavrilov, Pavel (Pavel Aleksandrovich), 1981- editor.
Title: Beyond the Siege of Leningrad : one woman's life during and after
   the occupation : the recollections of Evdokiia Vasil'evna
   Baskakova-Bogacheva / Evdokiia Vasil'evna Baskakova-Bogacheva ; edited
   by Oleg Beyda and Pavel Gavrilov.
Description: Budapest ; New York : Central European University Press, 2024.
   | Includes bibliographical references and index.
Identifiers: LCCN 2024000004 (print) | LCCN 2024000005 (ebook) | ISBN
   9789633867129 (hbk.) | ISBN 9789633867631 (pbk.) | ISBN 9789633867136 (pdf)
Subjects: LCSH: Saint Petersburg (Russia)--History--Siege, 1941-1944--Personal
   narratives, Russian. | World War, 1939-1945--Russia (Federation)--Pushkin--
   Personal narratives, Russian. | World War, 1939-1945--Women--Russia
   (Federation)--Pushkin--Biography. | World War, 1939-1945--Soviet Union--Medical
   care. | Women physicians--Soviet Union--Biography. | Pushkin (Russia)--
   Biography. | Pushkin (Russia)--History--20th century. | BISAC: BIOGRAPHY &
   AUTOBIOGRAPHY / Women | HISTORY / Russia / Soviet Era Classification:
   LCC D764.3.L4 B344 2024 (print) | LCC D764.3.L4 (ebook) |
   DDC 940.53092 [B]--dc23/eng/20240202
LC record available at https://lccn.loc.gov/2024000004
LC ebook record available at https://lccn.loc.gov/2024000005

CONTENTS

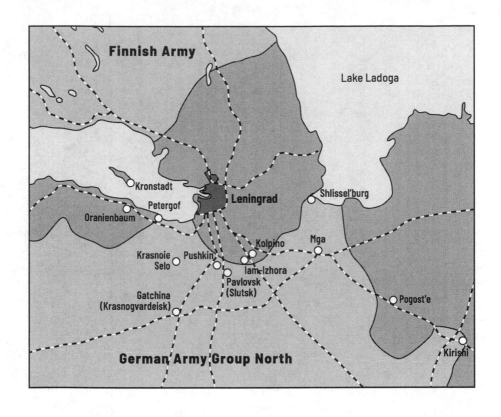

Figure 1. Map of Leningrad and its surroundings, 1941–43

Figure 2.
Map of Pushkin

Legend

1. Frontline
2. Moskovskoe Shosse
3. Moscow Gates
4. 7 Moskovskaia Ulitsa
5. Railway station
6. 1st School (former Realschule)
7. City hospital
8. First polyclinic on 13 Moskovskaia Ulitsa
9. Second polyclinic on Ulitsa Krasnoi Zvezdy
10. Residential building (former dormitory of the Agricultural Institute)
11. Knitwear factory
12. Automobile repair workshop (former imperial garages)
13. Mechanical works
14. Aleksandrovskii Palace
15. Ekaterininskii Palace
16. Znamenie Church
17. Institute of the Refrigeration and Milk Industry (Orangeries building)
18. Gostinyi Dvor
19. House of Culture
20. Kochubei mansion
21. Sofiiskii Cathedral

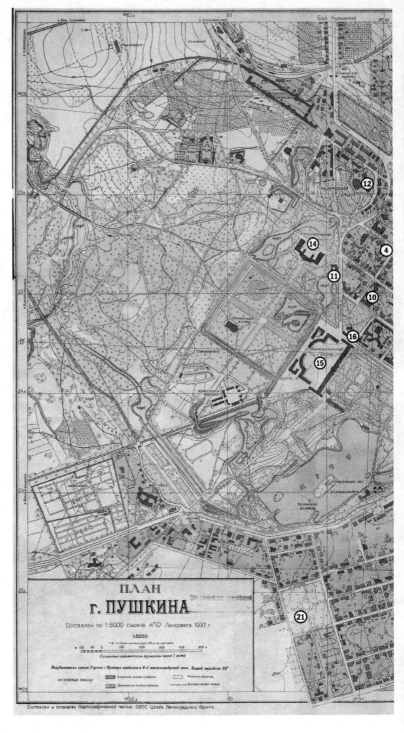

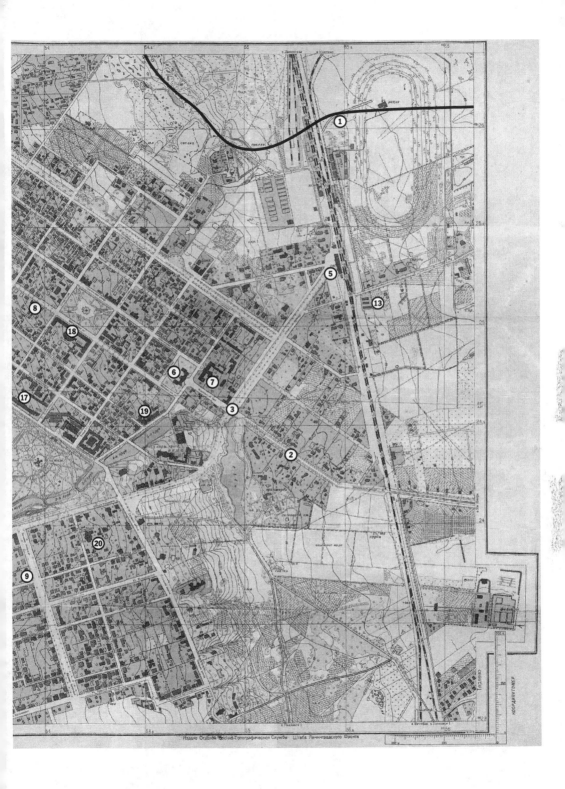

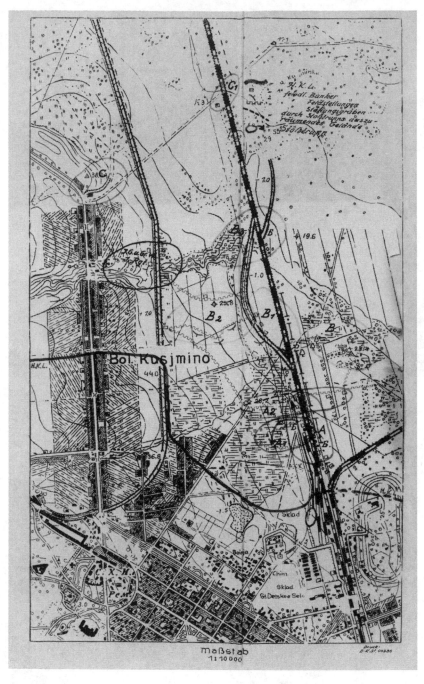

Figure 3. German military map of Pushkin (National Archives Record Administration, T-354 R-627 fr.000074).

INTRODUCTION

Beyond the Siege of Leningrad:
One Woman's Life during and after the Occupation

Oleg Beyda and Pavel Gavrilov

A hidden past

This memoir came from the pen of Evdokiia Vasil'evna Baskakova-Bogacheva (1888–1976), a medical practitioner and an émigré from the Soviet Union.[1] At the age of eighty-one, near the end of a checkered life that ended in Australia, she decided to set down her recollections on paper. She had an extraordinary tale to relate; in the depths of her past was a youth spent against the background of the First World War and the two Russian revolutions of 1917, followed by decades of work as a doctor, the hell of the Nazi occupation as experienced in a suburb of Leningrad, evacuation to Germany, emigration, and a new life on a remote continent. When she began to write, she had only six years left to live. She died on June 1, 1976, and was buried in the Orthodox section of Rookwood Cemetery in New South Wales.[2]

The writing of her memoir was prompted by a call issued in the émigré newspaper *Novoe Russkoe Slovo*, published in the USA, for members of the Russian emigration to record their memories, which would then be published in a combined history of Russia.[3] That appeal in February 1969 drew the attention of Evdokiia, and she devoted the year that followed to delving into her own past. She began a correspondence with the secretary of the Museum of Russian Culture in San Francisco, Andrei Naidenov, who persuaded her to send what she had written to the archive. Her manuscript, which, as may be seen from

---

[1]   The current work would not have been possible if not for the generous help of Professor Mark Edele who funded the translation of this source. The editors are very grateful to him and the University of Melbourne's School of Historical and Philosophical Studies (SHAPS).

[2]   Rookwood General Cemetery, Zone F—Russian Orthodox, O Section, Grave 193.

[3]   Pavel Perov, "Dostoinaia starost," *Novoe Russkoe Slovo*, no. 20425, February 8, 1969, 2.

the text, was incomplete and unedited, was deposited in the Museum on June 6, 1970.[4] Unfortunately, neither Naidenov's correspondence nor the ending of the text has been preserved (and the latter may not even have existed). In April 2020, we discovered the manuscript in the archive.[5]

Presented for your attention here is an émigré text written outside the geographical boundaries of Russia, and independently of the framework and culture that were devised in the USSR for recollections of the Second World War. This, however, is not the full extent of the "otherness" of the author's viewpoint. There is also a gender dynamic involved since our author was a woman. Intertwined with this is the unique role of a doctor in wartime, and moreover, of a doctor who was not practicing within the structures of an army, but who, between 1941 and 1943, was living in German-occupied Pushkin (Tsarskoe Selo).

This woman doctor was a civilian. Although our memories of the war are founded on the memoirs of people in uniform—for the most part, men—the global catastrophes of the last century affected tens of millions of ordinary people. Overwhelmingly, the human experience of the war consisted of *unarmed survival*, not of *armed resistance*, but this first type of experience has most often remained outside the narratives, and as it might seem, "on the sidelines" of the events of the past.

It is here that gender takes center stage. These recollections are brief and unpolished but are thus focused even more closely on the essence of what was occurring. Here we find a woman's view of a world run by men, an insider's perspective of the trauma and division caused by war. Baskakova's brief memoir describes the years from 1918 to 1920 and from 1941 to 1943—the most turbulent, bloody, romanticized, and sacred episodes of Soviet history. The people who managed to survive those years were mainly women who acted against a background of both an embodied emancipation and an archaic gender construct in society.

The occupation by the Germans of the USSR is also presented to us mainly through the testimonies of women, as there were simply more female survivors. The blockade of Leningrad is one of the few military topics in which the voices of women reverberate with deafening intensity. This has even allowed

---

[4] Communication from the Deputy Chairman of the Museum of Russian Culture, Yves Franquien, April 25, 2021.

[5] The Archive of the Museum of Russian Culture, San Francisco. The Manuscript Collection, Box 2, Folder 4. E. V. Bogacheva-Baskakova, untitled memoirs of life in Pushkin, USSR, under Nazi occupation, 1941–1944 [1969]. Holograph. We are grateful to Ivan Podvalov and Yves Franquien for their help in obtaining an electronic copy at the very beginning of the coronavirus crisis.

some authors to assert that the siege of the city was, for the most part, a female experience.[6] It is difficult to imagine a conversation about the siege without mention of Olga Berggol'ts, Vera Inber, or Lidiia Ginzburg. Or, without the diary of Tania Savicheva, a classic "Leningrad text" that has turned into a sacred artifact on a level with the writings of Anne Frank. Here, too, our source transgresses the usual bounds, resounding from outside the blockade the Soviet narrative and even the contemporary Russian language; Baskakova in the 1970s wrote in the way that people in Russia wrote in the 1900s. She survived for almost two years near the front lines, within a few kilometers of the blockade ring. Hers is thus a voice from the blockade, but *not entirely*, and it is stronger for the fact that she depicts, in a colorful manner, the nightmare of life under German rule in north-western Russia.

In the canon of the Soviet history of the war, a man is almost invariably a warrior with a passionate love of the Homeland, while a woman is assigned the role of a no less patriotic mother and the embodiment of enormous Grief. Baskakova's memoir operates outside these bounds. Her outlook embodies the collective memory of those who made up the silent majority, who are tongue-tied and who when they speak, express only the ideas of others. Here we may remember the common fate of the émigrés: in speaking of their exile from Russia, an exile that was superimposed on the trauma of the revolution, they would often find themselves resorting to the terms "previous" and "superfluous." The past, the "previous" that Baskakova recalls, takes on the same character—that of something awkward, unnecessary, unseemly, and even dangerous.

Meanwhile, sharp changes in tone were especially characteristic of Soviet citizens when they related their life stories and talked of the past. Two revolutions, the Civil War, the New Economic Policy (NEP) of the 1920s, collectivization, the Stalin regime, poorly understood and constantly changing icons and terms, the Great Terror, occupation, war, displaced persons camps—what was all that if not a series of ruptures and a constant changing of self-identification? Soviet citizens who had grown used to wearing masks were well-trained in social mimicry and in the art of radically refashioning their own past. It was possible, in order to survive in a society that changed with bewildering speed from campaign to campaign, both simply to conceal particular "inconvenient"

---

6   Cynthia Simmons, Nina Perlina, and Richard Bidlack, "Introduction," in *Writing the Siege of Leningrad: Women's Diaries, Memoirs, and Documentary Prose*, ed. Jonathan Harris (Pittsburgh, PA: University of Pittsburgh Press, 2002), 2.

facts about one's past and to completely alter one's identity.[7] Sheila Fitzpatrick, in her study of Soviet identity and imposture, uses the term *file-self*, a sort of "passportized identity" that might be invoked to demonstrate the bona fides of the individual, and which the latter always influenced.[8]

The gaps in people's biographies thus became a standard form of camouflage of the Russian past. Most colorful of all, within the context of a society that tortured itself with constant social engineering, were the chameleon-like impersonators, the "NEP people," who set out to beat the system. Playing this game amid the clamor of the Bolshevik agenda was an art that required not just cheek, but also a command of the language of the placard and the newspaper, a feel for the "official line," if only for the sake of carrying on activity outside the law. It is no accident that to this day, one of the most popular fictional characters in Russia is the "great manipulator" Ostap Bender— a dangerous trickster, fraud, cynical heartbreaker, and unprincipled contriver of illusions.[9]

Such "Benders," active opportunists driven by their thirst for enrichment, were, of course, the exception. Creative individuals are always in the minority, and most people do not create history; instead, history is something that happens to them. First, there are events, and then based on the totality of these events, the person who has fallen into the whirlpool rationalizes his or her own actions. The problem represented by this rationalization is crucial for the recollection of wars and other conflicts. It turns out that both atrocities and acts of self-sacrifice depend less on the qualities of the individual and on the nature of his or her desires than on the corridor of possibilities within which these qualities happen to manifest themselves. More simply, human beings are very restricted in the choices they have, while these choices exist in a chaotic expanse of a global or local catastrophe that is constantly changing. This is true in the case of any military conflict.[10]

---

[7] Golfo Alexopoulos, "Portrait of a Con Artist as a Soviet Man," *Slavic Review* 57, no. 4 (1998): 774–90; Aleida Assman, *Dlinnaia ten' proshlogo: memorial'naia kul'tura i istoricheskaia politika* (Moscow: Novoe literaturnoe obozrenie, 2014), 150–60.

[8] Sheila Fitzpatrick, *Tear Off the Masks! Identity and Imposture in 20th Century Russia* (Princeton and Oxford: Princeton University Press, 2005), 14.

[9] Sheila Fitzpatrick, "The World of Ostap Bender: Soviet Confidence Men in the Stalin Period," *Slavic Review* 61, no. 3 (2002): 535–57; Mark Lipovetsky, "Ostap Bender: The King is Born," in *Charms of the Cynical Reason: Tricksters in Soviet and Post-Soviet Culture* (Boston, MA: Academic Studies Press, 2011), 89–124.

[10] A striking example of such a personal reconfiguration prior to and during a war may be seen in the biography of Miletii Zykov, the ideologue of the Vlasov movement: Igor Petrov and Ivan Tolstoi, "Na svete nravstvennom zagadka," *Radio Liberty/Free Europe*, November 15, 2021, https://www.svoboda.org/a/na-svete-nravstvennom-zagadka/31561053.html.

The history of the siege of Leningrad reveals with exceptional clarity the contradictions between individual will, the surrounding chaos, and the *post factum* rationalizations that people make after events in their lives. However cynical this might appear, humanitarian catastrophes provide researchers with an abundance of material for studying the question of agency in history.[11] Here we come up against the topic not just of human choices but also of choices made under coercion, including coercion by a foreign power. The focus necessarily locks on the theme of collaborationism. Why did Soviet citizens resort to cooperating with the new authorities, with the Nazis, when there was no doubt that the Nazis were the enemy? Answers that attempt to explain these actions *solely* on the basis of hostility toward the Stalin regime are unsatisfying, nor do those that stress the low moral character of the collaborators reveal the essence of the question. So, why did collaboration occur? It is perhaps worth seeking an explanation in the simple banality of life beneath a foreign heel, since, as we recall, the experience of war is mostly a civilian matter rather than a military one.

We return once again to the theme of "invented biographies." Evdokiia Baskakova and her relatives belonged to the category of "former people" (*byvshie liudi*),[12] and were subjected to persecution by the Bolsheviks. Nevertheless, Evdokiia, as a doctor in a municipal polyclinic, and her engineer husband appeared by 1941 to be loyal and prosperous representatives of the nascent Soviet middle class, the "labor intelligentsia." The occupation did not leave such people with a great list of options; their jobs allowed them to survive, but this required collaboration with the enemy.[13]

---

[11]   Jeffrey K. Hass, *Wartime Suffering and Survival: The Human Condition under Siege in the Blockade of Leningrad, 1941–1944* (Oxford: Oxford University Press, 2021).

[12]   In the first instance, this term signified the old Russian aristocracy, but in practice it was used in a broader sense that included the class of "oppressors," to which anyone might be assigned who had enjoyed even minimal privileges in the old Russia. One might also be characterized in this way as a result of having been raised in the spirit of the old imperial ethic that placed great stress on etiquette and educated speech. Such mannerisms caused people to be assigned instantly to one camp in the sharp divide between new and old, and were often perceived by the Bolsheviks as distinguishing marks of "enemies." Douglas Smith, *Former People. The Final Days of the Russian Aristocracy* (New York: Picador, Farrar, Straus, and Giroux, 2013).

[13]   Aleksei Ivanovich Pliushkov ("Aleksei Ugriumov," "Aleksei Siverskii") suffered a similar fate. A former writer and legal consultant in prewar Pushkin, he had published his literary efforts and legal commentaries in the press. His writings included the obligatory, ritual invective aimed at "Trotskyist-Bukharinist degenerates." He was still in Pushkin when it came under occupation, and in the winter of 1942 his ten-year-old daughter fell ill and died. In 1943, Pliushkov was among the correspondents for the occupation press, receiving royalty payments from the propaganda department in Gatchina. He later became a lecturer at the University of Cambridge. A. I. Pliushkov, "Vozmezdie predateliam Rodiny," *Bol'shevistskoe Slovo*, no. 1, March 5, 1938. The same issue carried an analogous resolution on behalf of the staff at the Pushkin polyclinic where Baskako-

Once again, we find ourselves outside the frame of the usual black-and-white depictions. In the case of the Baskakov-Bogachev couple, there is no question of their being involved in the crimes of the German police or the Wehrmacht, but they could not be numbered among the stalwart members of the Resistance either. They inhabited a grey zone: working in civil institutions under the occupation could, at a minimum, be regarded as dubious, and at a maximum, as direct complicity in the functioning of a criminal authority. But was it a crime in itself? To place a moralizing stamp on such behavior does not explain the motives behind it; most likely, the actions concerned rested on the need of the people involved to survive and carry on with their everyday lives, just as under the Soviet regime. The Baskakov-Bogachevs and people like them thus accepted life under a totalitarian state and the inevitable compromises that had to be made with their consciences as being the rules of the game and not some kind of exception. These rules were multiplied by the surrounding chaos, and the game included an element of pure chance, with the moves depending on the "throw of the dice." For unpredictability, life under the Nazis may not have compared with life during the years of the Great Terror, but there was at least a degree of resemblance—uncertainty, multiplied by lethal danger on a day-to-day basis. Murder, fears for one's survival, treachery, mistrust, the use of special language, and the existence of social pariahs were all, to an extent, familiar elements of a well-known game, but one that in this case was far crueler and with higher stakes.

Portraits without faces

For the most part, all that we know of the biography of Evdokiia Vasil'evna Baskakova-Bogacheva is what she herself tells us. She was born in Moscow in 1888 to the family of the merchant Vasilii Semenovich Baskakov and was baptized in the Skorbiashchenskaia church on Ordynka Street.[14] The family was well off; the brothers Vasilii and Ivan, natives of the province of Vladimir, had

---

va worked; Amherst College, MA. Amherst Center for Russian Culture. The Archive Collection. The R. V. Ivanov-Razumnik Diary of 1942 (hereafter Amherst College/The Ivanov-Razumnik diary). Zapishnaia knizhka na 1942 god. 1/I. Tsarskoe Selo (Pushkin). Entry from January 20, 1942; Central State Archive of Saint-Petersburg (hereafter TsGA SPB). F. 3355. Op. 2. D. 1. L. 89, 92, 177. Prop.-Staffel Gatschina, O.U., August 30, 1943; Letter to the editor of the newspaper *Za Rodinu*, August 23, 1943; Prop.-Staffel Gatschina, O.U., May 10, 1943.

[14] Central State Historical Archive of Saint-Petersburg (hereafter TsGIA SPB). F. 436. Op. 1. D. 11511. L. 5. Metricheskoe svidetel'stvo E. V. Baskakovoi.

grown wealthy from construction contracts and owned substantial houses in Moscow.[15] Evdokiia had a brother, Aleksandr, and an older sister, Lidiia.

Evdokiia herself passed through the typical stages of women's education in that epoch: at the age of eight, she entered the Mariinskoe School, which prepared girls to work as home tutors, and later enrolled in the seventh class at the Third Moscow Women's Gymnasium. She completed her studies at the Gymnasium in 1906 and moved to St. Petersburg, where she began preparations to enter medical school, attending courses drawn up by Petr Frantsevich Lesgaft. In 1908, she enrolled in the Women's Medical Institute in St. Petersburg.[16]

Evdokiia's older, married sister was also living in the imperial capital. In 1912, Evdokiia herself was to be married to her sister's brother-in-law, Vladimir Bogachev. The Baskakov family were related in complex ways to the Bogachevs; two sisters married two brothers, and in the following generation, cousins from the two families married one another.

Evdokiia's husband, Vladimir Mikhailovich Bogachev, a descendant of the Kiev (Kyiv) hereditary nobility, was also a student, enrolled in the law faculty of St. Petersburg University. He too came from a large family; Evdokiia mentions two of his brothers, Georgii and Nikolai. Another brother, the railway official Anatolii Mikhailovich Bogachev, also figures in the archival sources. Like Vladimir, he studied at the First St. Petersburg Gymnasium. He was a marriage sponsor at the wedding of Evdokiia and Vladimir, and during the Second World War also lived in Pushkin.[17]

The young couple held relatively progressive views. Where religion was concerned, they embraced Tolstoyism,[18] and felt disdain for traditional values: "Earlier, we took the view that both children and parents were evils, with the only difference that children were an avoidable evil, while parents were an unavoidable one." Soon, however, reality began to catch up with even the most impudent theories. Evdokiia graduated with distinction from the medical in-

---

[15] From 1910, Vasilii lived in his own house at Degtiarnii Pereulok, dom 6. N. V. Bol'shakova, *Argunovskie mastera: V dvukh chastiakh; Chast' I* (Moscow: Kompaniia Sputnik, 2006), 185, 209, 214.

[16] TsGIA SPB. F. 436. Op. 1. D. 11511. L. 9. Zhenskii meditsinskii institut—lichnoe delo Baskakovoi-Bogachevoi Evdokii Vasil'evny.

[17] TsGIA SPB. F. 19. Op. 127. D. 3358. L. 50. Metricheskaia kniga tserkvi Sviatogo Chudotvortsa, selo Sablino, August 26, 1912; F. 1480. Op. 8. D. 665674. L. 1. Bogachev Anatolii, posluzhnoi spisok, 1916; F. 1480. Op. 9. D. 360. L.1, 23. Lichnoe delo Bogacheva Anatoliia Mikhailovicha; TsGA SPB. F. 8557. Op. 6. D. 1020. L. 267. Akty-spiski naseleniia goroda Pushkin, 1944.

[18] A social movement based on the religious and philosophical interpretations of Russian author Leo Tolstoy. It included a list of five principles, including those of loving your enemies, avoiding anger, fighting evil with good, and not taking any oaths.

stitute in May 1914.[19] Ahead of her was the last summer of peace. The empire was now striding, in the words of George Kennan, toward "the great seminal catastrophe of the twentieth century," a world war.

After graduating from the institute, Evdokiia worked as a doctor in the Aleksandrovskaia community of the Russian Red Cross. With the beginning of the First World War, the Russian Red Cross came to act as the main reserve of female medical personnel for the army, and was transformed into a powerful, well-administered organization. In post-revolutionary Russia, however, it was gradually smothered along with the free trade unions.[20] Medical personnel were subject to mobilization, and so it was that Evdokiia Bogacheva was sent off to military service in May 1917, after the fall of the Tsar in the February Revolution.[21]

Judging from her recollections, she felt no patriotism whatsoever. Her writings on this period deal with the months of revolutionary collapse and describe mainly her efforts to return home from the hospital in Rzhev to which she had been posted. After going on leave, she tried by all means, both legitimate and illegitimate, to delay going back; she recounts how overjoyed she was, on arriving home, to fall ill with typhus, the very disease that during those years took several million lives. Evdokiia managed finally to leave military service behind her only in 1920, due to pregnancy: "I had to provide myself [with a son] in order to save myself from being drafted for military service during the Civil War." Displaying the same openness, she describes how she performed an operation to cripple her husband; to save Vladimir from mobilization, she partly severed his Achilles tendon.

The couple's unwillingness to go to the Civil War front is understandable, especially if her Tolstoian views are taken into account. These beliefs, meanwhile, did not signify a complete rejection of the new regime. The Baskakov-Bogachevs sought to take advantage of the opportunities provided by the revolution; Evdokiia describes how she took part in conferences of Red Cross workers and was even among the delegates to the Petrograd Congress of Workers Deputies. She never made a party or Soviet career for herself, but the *obshchestvennitsa*,[22] the public-spirited woman, was to remain a part of her identity.

---

[19] TsGIA SPB. F. 436. Op. 4. D. 320. L. 12. Lichnoe delo Baskakovoi Evdokii Vasil'evny.

[20] A. V. Sribnaia, *Sestry miloserdiia v gody Pervoi mirovoi voiny* (Moscow: Izd-vo TSTGU, 2017).

[21] Russian State Military Archive (hereafter RGVA). Kartoteka na vybyvshikh, 7412-A. Elekronnaia kopiia: https://gwar.mil.ru/heroes/chelovek_gospital2133095.

[22] A female activist. The term usually refers to women engaged in socially useful activities. It became a formalized movement in the late 1930s.

Her husband, Vladimir, who never became a lawyer, had begun working as a railway agent while he was still a student. Then, until 1918, he was employed as a clerk and bookkeeper in the office of the firm "Rabotnik," a brokerage enterprise supplying agricultural machinery.[23] During the stormy years of civil slaughter, Vladimir spent time as a clerk in various offices; during the period of War Communism,[24] he and his wife attempted to preserve the hospital of the Aleksandrovskaia community, of which he even became the administrator. During the relative economic relaxation of the 1920s, when the Bolsheviks allowed for a limited and controlled quasi-market economy to exist, known as the NEP years, he managed the "Anons" private cinema on Karl Marx Prospekt in Leningrad. In 1925, he was granted a private business license.[25]

In the early 1920s, the couple settled in Pushkin, where they bought a private house. This was possible only on the condition of carrying out necessary repairs to the building. In 1927, as pressures increased on the remaining elements of private property, they were forced to surrender the house to the municipal authorities. Baskakova indicates that it ultimately came to be occupied by the writer Viacheslav Shishkov. After the NEP was wound up, Vladimir Bogachev left his managerial career and took on a more suitable job in the "Metalloshtamp" metal stamping workshop. From 1928 at the latest, Evdokiia worked as a surgeon in the provincial polyclinic of the water transport authority in Leningrad and, from an uncertain date, in the Pushkin municipal polyclinic.[26]

The couple enjoyed astonishing good fortune in negotiating all the death traps on the road that led to the imposition of the Stalinist order. There was just one exception: in 1930, the Pushkin municipal commission put Vladimir Bogachev on its list of people who had been deprived of their electoral rights—a Soviet way of social assassination, usually reserved for those who belonged to the former "oppressive classes." The pretext was the letting of the couple's house; formally speaking, Bogachev as the landlord was subject to income tax, that is, he had received unearned income.[27] The situation was exacerbated by

---

[23] TsGA SPB. F. 9133. Op. 1. D. 23. L. 12, 17. Posluzhnoi spisok Vladimira Bogacheva, December 20, 1930; Zaiavlenie Vladimira Bogacheva v pushkinskuiu gorodskuiu komissiiu po delam lisheniia izbiratel'nykh prav, December 20, 1930; *Ves' Petrograd na 1917 god* (Petrograd: A. S. Suvorin, 1917), 67.

[24] The economic and political system that existed in Sovietized parts of the former Russian Empire from 1918 until 1921.

[25] TsGA SPB. F. 1963. Op. 1a. D. 95b. L. 167. Patent Bogacheva V. M. ot 2 marta 1925; F. 1963. Op. 1a. D. 99. L. 15. Patent Bogacheva V. M. ot 1 ianvariia 1925.

[26] *Ves' Leningrad i Leningradskaia oblast': adresnaia i spravochnaia kniga na 1930 god. Chast' 1. Ves' Leningrad* (Leningrad, 1928), 216.

[27] TsGA SPB. F. 9133. Op. 1. D. 9. L. 1–17. Delo o lishenii izbiratel'nykh prav Bogacheva V. M., December 20, 1930–January 26, 1931.

the fact that Vladimir had a dangerous family connection: his brother, the former officer of the Life Guards Georgii Bogachev, had already been arrested several times by the beginning of the 1930s. In 1935, Georgii was exiled to Kazakhstan, and in 1938, he was shot.

The threat to Vladimir's life was very real. When he and Evdokiia had been married in 1912 there had been four sponsors at the ceremony, two of whom, Staff Captain Georgii Bogachev and Nikolai Ivanovich Negri, would not survive the Great Terror of 1937–38, otherwise known as "the purges," a campaign of terror when hundreds of thousands of undesirables were executed, and millions thrown in jails and fed to the vast camp system.[28] By an irony of fate, Nikolai Negri's son Vissarion also lived in Pushkin, became an activist of the Communist Party, and during the war was a commissar in a partisan detachment. After the war, he worked successfully in the party's regional committee. He had almost no recollection of his father, who had abandoned him when he was an infant.[29]

The peak danger time of the "purges" thus passed the Baskakov-Bogachev couple by, leaving them unharmed. Vladimir proved at his second attempt that he had not received unearned income, and in February 1931, his rights were restored. He managed to fit into a Soviet society that was once again in the process of transforming itself. Receiving a new higher education, he began serving the state as an engineer,[30] finding refuge in an institution with the sonorous title "North-Western Office of the Main Supply Department of the People's Commissariat of the Building Materials Industry."

Maintaining a studious silence about his past, this son of the aristocracy did well in his job. We find his name in the office's report for 1939 on socialist competition, mentioned among the "comrades performing in shock-worker fashion."[31] His wife, too, was well regarded in her workplace, and in 1939 was even chosen as a deputy to the city soviet.[32] In 1940, their son graduated from

---

[28] Prior to the revolution, Negri, like Anatolii Bogachev, had been a railway official. During the First World War, Negri had been mobilized, had graduated from a school for warrant officers, and after the revolution, like Georgii Bogachev, had served in the Red Army, on the staff of the 7th Army. In the mid-1930s, he was arrested. Later, he served as manager of the Starorusskii Distillery, and lived in the town of Staraya Russa. In October 1937, he was shot. *Kniga Pamiati zhertv politicheskikh repressii Novgorodskoi oblasti*, vol. 1: 296. Elektronnyi resurs: http://lists.memo.ru/d24/fl78.htm.

[29] Central State Archive of Historical-Political Documents of Saint-Petersburg (hereafter TsGAIPD SPB). F. 1788. Op. 1. D. 624857. L. 2. Avtobiografiia Negri Vissariona Nikolaevicha, 1933.

[30] National Archives of Australia (hereafter NAA). A12029, 682–683, Barcode 4763428. PCIRO Resettlement Registration Form, Emigration to Australia, Area 3. Bogatschew Wladimir, February 15, 1950.

[31] TsGAIPD SPB. F. 408. Op. 1. D. 748. L. 80. "Doklad tov. Pokrass o deiatel'nosti S-3 kontory Glavsnaba za 1939 g.," February 16, 1940.

[32] TsGA SPB. F. 4958. Op. 1. D. 32. L. 74–75. Stenograficheskii otchet zasedaniia 1-i sessii Pushkinskogo raisoveta, February 1, 1940.

the 10th class of the Pushkin school and took part in a public discussion in the press. As part of a public "criticism and self-criticism" episode of the kind that is typical of totalitarian culture, the city newspaper published comments on a problem student in a local school; the young Vladimir weighed in with an appeal to give the student one more chance.[33] Before the war began, the younger Vladimir managed to begin studies at a technical institute.[34] At the time when the Nazis invaded the USSR in June 1941, the Baskakov-Bogachev family—progressive-minded, working in practical professions, active in civic affairs, living in an apartment in a suburb of Leningrad—appeared almost like a model unit of the new society.

Evdokiia Baskakova relates how, after the beginning of the war, she worked as a doctor in a military call-up commission. By an irony of fate, the future burgomaster of the city of Pushkin, Mikhail Urtaev, had entered the same commission in January 1941.[35] That same year, the 20-year-old Vladimir junior was due to be conscripted into the armed forces, but late in July 1941, on the very day after he received his draft notice, he fell ill and finished up being declared unfit for military service.[36] We may surmise that the "illness" was merely a cunning ruse, and that the outcome had been prompted by the young man's mother.

In the shadow of the blockade

On September 17, 1941, units of the SS Police Division (*SS-Polizei-Division*) and the 269th Infantry Division entered Pushkin. The occupation had begun, and for the next two and a half years the front was literally within a few hundred meters of the city's northern boundary. The Baskakov-Bogachevs lived in the zone of military action until early 1943 and finished up among the "long-term residents," those whom the occupiers transferred last of all from the zone marked for evacuation. Once again, the couple adapted, making use of the only thing they could rely on—their professional skills.

---

33 V. Baskakov, "Neispravimykh uchenikov net," *Bol'shevistskoe Slovo*, no. 29 (306), March 10, 1940, 4.

34 NAA. A11703, 432–433, Barcode 5161562. IRO Resettlement Registration Form, Emigration to Australia, Area 3. Bogatschew Wladimir, January 11, 1949.

35 TsGAIPD SPB. F. 2242. Op. 1. D. 515. L. 4. Materialy po voennoi rabote v Pushkinskom raione, January 1–31, 1941.

36 Central Archive of the Ministry of Defense of the Russian Federation (hereafter TsAMO RF). Kartoteka Leningradskogo voenno-peresyl'nogo punkta. Op. 530157. D. 42740. L. 311. Registratsionnaia kartochka No. 11817, August 8, 1941.

Evdokiia worked in her profession as a doctor. Her husband, as an engineer, headed a knitwear factory organized by the 121st Infantry Division of the Wehrmacht to meet its needs; the factory was located on the territory of the Soviet "Second Five-Year Plan Works," in the kitchen block of the Aleksandrovskii Palace. The couple's son and daughter-in-law also survived. The pay records for April 1942 list V. V. Baskakov and M. I. Baskakova—the younger Vladimir and his future wife Mariia, whose maiden name was Evgrasheva.[37] We know that Evdokiia Baskakova had a daughter-in-law only from immigration documents. The younger Baskakov-Bogachevs also settled in Australia, and a form states that the marriage took place in 1943. That is logical; Mariia Evgrasheva was born in 1925, and in the spring of 1942 she was only 17 years old.[38] Evdokiia does not mention her son's wife at all, which prompts a banal assumption: Evdokiia did not approve of the marriage, and her relations with her young daughter-in-law were strained.

The population of Pushkin was supposed to be removed from the zone of military operations, but in practice, the evacuation dragged on for almost a year. Even after this, workers in enterprises that were needed by the occupiers remained in the city, living in barracks. The Baskakov-Bogachev couple were in this "necessary" category; hence, Vladimir, after ceasing to be employed in the knitwear factory, worked in automobile repair workshops. They succeeded in leaving the front-line suburb in March 1943, and then, after a further period spent close to the frontlines, departed for Germany.

Baskakova's text breaks off after an account of life in Elizavetino near Gatchina, but preserved among documents relating to the rear of Army Group North is a list of local people of German ancestry (*Volksdeutsche*) who were evacuated. A certain *Evgeniia* Baskakova-Bogacheva and her husband Vladimir were among those who, on October 27, 1943, were sent to the Danzig district from an assembly point in Pskov.[39] This was the result of another fiction, an adept move in the quest for survival. In her memoirs, Evdokiia briefly mentions a colleague, the neuropathologist Dr. B., who managed to pass himself off as a German and leave Pushkin. It is quite obvious that in her case, a similar

---

[37] TsGA SPB. F. 3355. Op. 10. D. 32. L. 7. Vedomost' na vydachu zarplaty rabochim trikotazhnoi fabriki, April 15, 1942. At his birth, Vladimir was given his mother's surname, in later documents he appears as Baskakov-Bogachev.

[38] NAA. A11703, 432–433, Barcode 5161562. IRO Resettlement Medical Examination Form. Bogatschew Maria, June 17, 1949.

[39] The National Archives and Records Administration, Washington DC (hereafter NARA). T-311. R. 115. Fr. 7154752, 7154765. Der Komandierende General der Sicherungstruppen und Befehlshaber im Heeresgebiet Nord, VII 729/43 g. An OKdo H GR Nord-OQu/VII, November 24, 1943.

backdoor maneuver was successful later on, even though the family was completely lacking in German ancestry.

Until 1944, the couple stayed in a camp in the Pomeranian village of Klintsch,[40]
and then moved to Berensdorf, where Evdokiia worked as a camp physician.[41]
The younger Baskakov-Bogachevs finished up in Berensdorf as well. From 1945
to 1949, they lived in Kolitzheim, and in the summer of 1949 applied to emigrate
to Australia. To improve their chances of survival, they once again resorted to
a maneuver; this time, they took advantage of the fact that Vladimir Bogachev
senior had been born in Kiev. Evdokiia, her husband, her son, and daughter-
in-law declared themselves to be Ukrainians. They were not, but such origins
could speed the granting of a visa in the displaced persons camps.[42] The younger
Baskakov-Bogachevs were the first to migrate, in July 1949, to be followed in
1950 by the parents.[43] In June 1958 Evdokiia received Australian citizenship.[44]

Typical untypical

We should note not only Baskakova's retentive memory but also how credible her
text is. All the events she recalls can be confirmed through other sources. Most of
the people she mentions can be identified from archives as having actually existed.
Unfortunately, there is something that cannot be established: the extremely interesting but, for the present, unclear fates of the numerous members of the Baskakov-Bogachev extended family. There are also plenty of gaps in the biography of
the author and main heroine. Her silence on this or that topic might be considered
dubious, and hypotheses could be ventured on that basis, but there are no guarantees that the reason is not far simpler: that her writings were left unfinished,
and that her pen simply followed where the stream of her memory flowed most
quickly. One can hardly expect a full treatment of the subject, and a sense of com-
pleteness, in the memoir of an 80-year-old who had never written professionally.

---

[40] Now Wielki Klincz in Poland, some 50 kilometers south of Gdańsk.

[41] NAA. A12029, 682–683, Barcode 4763428. PCIRO Resettlement Registration Form, Emigration
to Australia, Area 3. Bogatschew Ewdokija, February 15, 1950.

[42] Sheila Fitzpatrick, *White Russians, Red Peril: A Cold War History of Migration to Australia* (Melbourne: La Trobe University Press, in conjunction with Black Inc., 2021), 59.

[43] Online Archive of the Bad Arolsen Archives, Registration and files of Displaced Persons, Children and
Missing Persons, Evidence of Abode and Emigration—Emigrations, Reference Code 8314720. https://col-
lections.arolsen-archives.org/en/search/person/81764688?s=Bogatschew%20Vladimir&t=24680&p=1.

[44] *Commonwealth of Australia Gazette.* Published by authority. Canberra, Thursday, October 30, 1958,
no. 66, 3664. Bogatchev (formerly Bogatschew), Evdokya, an entry from June 10, 1958.

In our work, we have again and again asked ourselves the inevitable question: How typical was her history? Can the assessments she provides be relied on? When one works with personal recollections, archival materials should be used after the event to reliably counterbalance the subjective judgments. Nevertheless, between the "hard data" of the archives and the "soft" reflections of a memoirist, there remains a margin of the unknown. Should the actions of the Baskakov-Bogachev couple in the USSR be considered deliberate mimicry or adaptation? Has the standard of behavior that the person is supposed to imitate changed as well? The problem is that, contrary to the widespread stereotype, not even a war can serve as a "moment of truth." War does not reveal a person's "essence" (if such a thing even exists) but is only able to illuminate one or another facet of his or her personality.

For example, one could conclude that the Baskakov-Bogachevs stayed in Pushkin deliberately, counting on being saved from the Bolsheviks, despite their previous relatively successful lives under the Soviets. Speaking of the beginning of the catastrophe of 1941, Evdokiia writes of the prevailing "joyful excitement, artfully concealed behind a mask of anxious preoccupation and a decent degree of fuss and bustle." Historians are indeed aware that there were defeatist moods in Leningrad, as recorded in the summaries of the NKVD.[45] By the autumn of 1941, a change of regime seemed for many to be simply inevitable. On August 20, the worker Ivan Kharichev, who lived not far from Pushkin and who joined the partisans, noted in his diary that local women were threatening to denounce his wife and other wives of communists once the Germans arrived.[46] A new pattern of daily life had begun.

Questions of everyday life are above all pragmatic in nature, and people decided whether to evacuate based on what seemed to them more threatening—the approaching occupiers or the loss of their homes and means of existence. From a pragmatic point of view, people during the occupation engaged in many of the same activities that had consumed their lives during previous years: *paikolovstvo*, the securing of rations; searches for somewhere to live, under the conditions of enforced communal housing; barter; and corruption.[47]

---

[45] N. A. Lomagin, *V tiskakh goloda: Blokada Leningrada v dokumentakh germanskikh spetssluzhb, NKVD i pis'makh leningradtsev*, 2nd ed. (Saint-Petersburg: Avrora-Dizain, 2014), 179–81.

[46] NARA. T-312. R. 794. Fr. 8448370. Dnevnik partizana Kharicheva (July–September 1941). Entry from August 20, 1941.

[47] James Heinzen, *The Art of the Bribe: Corruption under Stalin, 1943–1953* (New Haven and London: Yale University Press, 2016).

Once again, we come up against the question of choice and of differing reactions within a formally totalitarian society, even if it was one in the process of collapse. In recent research on the political culture of Stalinism, Olga Velikanova showed that the Stalinist USSR was home to a whole spectrum of attitudes, from liberal to conservative. Together with the multilevel internal divisions of society, this gave rise to bizarre combinations: a defense in principle of the state system might be combined with sharp criticism of specific actions of the elites, and a faith in socialism combined with cynical mockery of its Russian version.[48] A diversity of views certainly existed in the USSR, but it was always combined with a panicked and visceral fear of disagreements, something that created in citizens an uneasy sense of living in a besieged fortress. This created an attitude toward life in which people longed to speak out but thought it better to keep their mouths shut tight, reasoning that now was not the time. Voicing one's thoughts was often dangerous because the agenda changed regularly and dramatically. Typically, life before the war thus involved tense expectations and survival in a "grey zone" where every step might retrospectively be proclaimed as treason. Obviously, this experience also weighed on people as they tried to survive the war years. It is not surprising that such mental somersaults eventually led to the hypocrisy, double-think, and pervasive cynicism that tore late-Soviet society apart.[49]

"Mental disobedience," however, could also find expression in the conditions of silence. One of the forms of this disobedience might be the writing of a personal text.

Speaking Anti-Bolshevik

Baskakova's writings are neither literary works nor are they complete. There is no sign that her text ever received the attention of an editor, and we see this as an advantage, since it shows the pulsation of the author's living thought.

But in the case of a memoir, who, properly speaking, is doing the remembering, and what is it that he or she remembers? These two questions must be asked, since memoirs as a genre are very diverse. From testimony in a court case to

---

[48]   Olga Velikanova, *Mass Political Culture under Stalinism: Popular Discussion of the Soviet Constitution of 1936* (Cham: Palgrave Macmillan, 2018).

[49]   Alexei Yurchak, *Everything Was Forever, until It Was No More: The Last Soviet Generation* (Princeton, NJ: Princeton University Press, 2006); Oleg Kharkhordin, *Oblichat' i litsemerit': genealogiia rossiiskoi lichnosti* (Saint-Petersburg: Izdatel'stvo Evropeiskogo universiteta v Sankt-Peterburge, 2016).

the utterance of a symbol of faith, memoirs are *testimony*, in all its breadth and depth of meaning. In the case we are dealing with here, close to thirty years elapsed between the time when the events occurred and when they were described, and to define the author's exact position is difficult. We do not know enough about Evdokiia to say with any certainty what she was in fact thinking; we know rather little about her convictions. Nevertheless, we can attempt, by feeling our way, to gain a sense of the position that the text itself occupies in relation to other texts of a similar kind.

What external framework can be defined for our source, and what is its starting point? What milieu does it inhabit? The text belongs to the category of first-hand accounts. Thematically, it straddles two provinces: testimonies concerning the German occupation, and those on life in Leningrad during the Second World War. As was mentioned earlier, Baskakova survived the blockade along with the city, living outside its boundary but sufficiently close to be scorched by the fire of German occupation policy.

The blockade of Leningrad thus towers over the narrative, and the suburb of Pushkin lies within the orbit of this catastrophe. Hunger, discord, disease, the hunt for food and firewood, along with violence and death—everything that our heroine describes revolves in one way or another around the two sieges of the city, during the Civil War and in the period of the German-Soviet war, in 1919 and from 1941.

There is already a whole body of literature devoted to first-hand accounts of the blockade.[50] Further, there exists a whole body of texts created by witnesses to the occupation of the Leningrad suburbs. In the case of Pushkin, these were written by people who knew one another or who knew of one another. Baskakova's memoirs are of value not just as a unique object but also as one more piece of the puzzle.

The people who remained in Pushkin during the occupation included some who left a notable trace in history: the Soviet writer Vera Panova; one of the pioneers of Soviet science fiction, Aleksandr Beliaev; and the Russian literary scholar and sociologist Razumnik Vasil'evich Ivanov-Razumnik. Their fates embody the main variants in the paths of Russian intellectuals—a successful pro-Soviet orientation, death, or emigration. Panova remained in the USSR and

---

[50] A recent project is a library of blockade diaries, of which the first volume appeared in 2021, see A. I. Pavlovskaia and N. A. Lomagin, eds., *"Ia znaiu, chto tak pisat' nel'zia": Fenomen blokadnogo dnevnika* (Saint-Petersburg: Izdatel'stvo Evropeiskogo universiteta v Sankt-Peterburge, 2021); A. F. Pavlovskii and N. A. Lomagin, eds., *"Vy, naverno, iz Leningrada?": Dnevniki evakuirovannykh iz blokadnogo goroda* (Saint-Petersburg: Izdatel'stvo Evropeiskogo universiteta v Sankt-Peterburge, 2023).

received three Stalin Prizes, Beliaev died of hunger in the winter of 1942, and Ivanov-Razumnik during the same winter was evacuated to Germany, where he died in Munich after the war. Panova wrote a memoir, while Ivanov-Razumnik from the winter of 1942 kept a diary.[51] There are testimonies by relatives of Beliaev; his daughter Svetlana left reminiscences.[52]

It is worth recalling the diary of the adolescent Liusia Khordikainen (Iuliia Krivulina).[53] The Khordikainen family were also members of the intelligentsia and acquaintances of Ivanov-Razumnik. In the published text very little is said about the occupation of Pushkin, but this source provides a view from the perspective of someone who as a teenager experienced the trauma of the occupation, and also the trauma of returning to Soviet society.

Other available eyewitness accounts are collected in the book by Vladimir Tsypin *Gorod Pushkin v gody voiny* (The city of Pushkin during the war years). This has the character of a local history but is more informative.[54] It is also necessary to mention one of the fundamental sources on the history of the occupation of north-western Russia, the collection compiled by Izol'da Ivanova *Za blokadnym kol'tsom* (Beyond the blockade ring).[55]

Evdokiia Baskakova personally mentions a number of testimonies. As already explained, the story of her text began with an appeal that was included in an essay by Pavel Perov, written in the spirit of memory studies. Published by the newspaper *Novoe Russkoe Slovo*, Perov's essay combined the themes of the émigrés' personal memories that were vanishing with people's inevitable deaths; of social memory that was departing with assimilation and the change of generations; and cultural memory, that is, "the common bank of materials" that preserved 50 years of the life of the exiles for their descendants and for future researchers.

Appearing on the same page of the newspaper was a text that bore directly on the blockade of Leningrad—fragments from the creative activity of Anatolii Darov (Dukhonin). Darov was another émigré with an involved fate. An eye-

---

51 Vera Panova, *Moio i tol'ko moio: O moei zhizni, knigakh i chitateliakh* (Saint-Petersburg: Zhurnal "Zvezda," 2005); Amherst College/The Ivanov-Razumnik diary.

52 S. A. Beliaeva, "Vozvrashchaias' k proshlomu," in *Ivanov-Razumnik: Lichnost'; Tvorchestvo; Rol' v kul'ture* (Saint-Petersburg: V. Belous, 1996), 39–43; S. A. Beliaeva, *Vospominaniia ob ottse* (Saint-Petersburg: Serebrianyi vek, 2009). Beliaev's wife and daughter were also evacuated to Germany, and after the end of the war spent 11 years in exile in the Altai District.

53 S. A. Nuridzhanova, ed., *Zhizn' v okkupatsii i pervye poslevoennye gody: Pushkin-Gatchina-Estoniia; Dnevnik Liusi Khordikainen* (Saint-Petersburg: Nestor-Istoriia, 2011).

54 V. Tsypin, *Gorod Pushkin v gody voiny* (Saint-Petersburg: Genio Loci, 2019).

55 I. A. Ivanova, ed., *Za blokadnym kol'tsom: Sbornik vospominanii zhitelei Leningradskoi oblasti vremen germanskoi okkupatsii 1941–1944 gg.* (Saint-Petersburg: Vesti, 2010).

witness to the deadly Leningrad winter of 1941–1942 who had subsequently evacuated only to become a collaborator, he was later the author of a novel entitled *The Blockade*,[56] which appeared in New York but was never published in the USSR. Chapters from his novel *Bessmertniki* (The Immortals), published "to mark the 25th anniversary of the breaking of the Leningrad blockade," are full of religious allusions and describe Leningrad as "the apocalypse," a city of the living dead and of the dead living.[57] Baskakova could not have failed to read these chapters, despite personally being remote from religion—her text is exclusively secular.

The Leningrad catastrophe became one of the dominant features of Soviet and post-Soviet historical memory. For studying the phenomenon of late-Soviet historical writing, Tat'iana Voronina has introduced the concept of "socialist realist historicism."[58] For the text of the émigré Baskakova, this whole complex of images and ideas makes up only an outer boundary, and for all the resemblance to the extreme war experience, what our heroine experienced was precisely the occupation.

Are we, then, able to classify Baskakova's text? A famous historian of Stalinism, Stephen Kotkin, devised the concept of *speaking Bolshevik*—a virtue-signaling way of expressing oneself in a highly politicized domain. Those who adopted the new Bolshevik vernacular and mastered the imposed duckspeak had a better chance at climbing the social hierarchy while simultaneously indoctrinating others. Those who abstained or persisted without the new vocabulary fell through the social cracks.[59] This Soviet verbal conformity took on literary forms that persisted after the war. The mental assimilation of the wartime experience was expressed in the forms of heroism, self-sacrifice, grief, and treachery suggested by the Soviet system itself. This means that a socialist-realist cluster of literature dealing with the blockade, a *Soviet* "Leningrad text," existed as well. Within this text, the city's people, exhausted by hunger but believing in the victory of the forces of good and in the triumph of Leninist ideas, were invariably shining examples of humanity, self-sacrificing by nature, steadfast and mighty amid the unprecedented catastrophe that had

---

[56] On Darov as an observer of the Leningrad catastrophe, see Polina Barskova, *Sed'maia shcheloch': Teksty i sud'by blokadnykh poetov* (Saint-Petersburg: Izdatel'stvo Ivana Limbakha, 2020), 82–87.

[57] A. Darov, "K 25-letiiu proryva blokady Leningrada," *Novoe Russkoe Slovo*, no. 20425, February 8, 1969, 2–3.

[58] T. Voronina, *Pomnit' po-nashemu: Sotsrealisticheskii istorizm i blokada Leningrada* (Moscow: Novoe Literaturnoe Obozrenie, 2018).

[59] Stephen Kotkin, *Magnetic Mountain: Stalinism as a Civilization* (Berkeley: University of California Press, 1995), 198–237.

befallen them, and always united in the face of the enemy.[60] This narrative is alive to this day and is the main, official, public means of relating the story of the Leningrad tragedy.

There was, however, also the phenomenon of *speaking anti-Bolshevik*. This took the form of an *anti-Soviet* "Leningrad text." Wafting from its pages was the stench of the dead bodies that littered the streets, and that were devoured by packs of stray dogs. In the dying city of two revolutions, only heartless Bolshevist bosses were sleek and plump; they gorged themselves on caviar and other delicacies while mocking the apathetic, suffering population.[61] The Germans and their responsibility for the murder of an entire city were placed in parenthesis, while the shelling was described in detached terms, like inclement weather. Born on the pages of the Russian-language occupation press, this "Leningrad text" survived in its pure form for only a few years before smashing into the victory of the Red Army in 1945.[62] Nevertheless, the sharp fragments of the propagandist arguments concerning the blockade left their trace. Pieces of the shattered discourse were preserved in emigration, and in the form of sharp-edged attitudes and ideas, even returned to post-Soviet Russia, where this counter-narrative managed to take root in numerous spaces that had been left empty by the official Soviet version of history.

It is certain that Evdokiia encountered this second text that was created in the emigration, and this would have encouraged her to set down her own truth, one that did not fall into either of the two categories. The catalyst for her was the "diary of a collaborator" kept by Olimpiada Poliakova ("Lidiia Osipova")— a relatively well-known source, the work of an impassioned woman who served the Nazis. In Pushkin, she and her husband occupied a social position bordering on the milieu of the intelligentsia. At one point, the couple had even shared a dwelling with Vera Panova, and they were acquainted with Ivanov-Razumnik and his wife. Baskakova and Poliakova were neighbors during the occupation, living in adjacent streets. They provide recollections of the same people, though they were not acquainted personally.

---

[60] On the narrative of the blockade in Soviet literature, see Evgenii Dobrenko, "Blokada real'nosti: Leningradskaia tema v sotsrealizme," in *Blokadnye narrativy*, ed. P. Barskova and R. Nikolozi (Moscow: Novoe Literaturnoe Obozrenie, 2017), 20–46; Lisa A. Kirschenbaum, *The Legacy of the Siege of Leningrad, 1941–1995: Myth, Memories, and Monuments* (Cambridge: Cambridge University Press, 2006).

[61] "Chelovek iz Leningrada," *Za Rodinu*, no. 66 (161), March 20, 1943, 4.

[62] Boris Ravdin, "Blokada Leningrada v russkoi podnemetskoi pechati 1941–1945 godov," in Barskova and Nikolozi, *Blokadnye narrativy*, 274–313.

The reaction of our author is perfectly understandable. Poliakova's writings agitate the reader; in evidence there is her emotionalism, even hysteria, as well as the backhanded but also, in reality, ardently self-justifying image of the "interior emigrant." The manuscript of these diary entries has not been discovered, and as the research of Oleg Budnitskii shows, the original writings of diarists were substantially reworked before publication.[63] This does not mean that Poliakova's text is unreliable—all the details mentioned in it can be confirmed—but the center of the narrative is Poliakova herself and her constant struggle with the entire world (including her struggle to promote her own image).

Baskakova in many ways takes her lead from Poliakova, but with a fundamental difference. Poliakova was a postwar émigré essayist who needed a "smoothed-out" biography for the projection of her ideas. She needed to be "cleaned up" in the eyes of her associates and supporters, members of the émigré National Labor Alliance (NTS), who adhered to the concept of a "third force." Even the title "Diary of a Collaborator" speaks to the fact that she was publishing her views at a time when the idea of "collaborationism" was considered unpleasant, and as needing somehow to be explained. Poliakova does this by way of the idea of the "third force"—a sort of anti-Soviet Russian patriotism, incomprehensible to the Germans, that permitted collaboration with Hitler in order to advance the struggle against Stalin, while not necessarily sharing the politics of the former. The narrative corresponds to its name; the supporters of the "third force" were people who had inherently rejected the Soviet regime long before the Germans arrived. It was precisely for this reason that they had expected the occupiers to bring them freedom, and had found themselves cruelly deceived; nevertheless, they had continued to believe in their principles and, to the extent possible, waged a fight against injustice and for their honest ideals of a pure anti-Bolshevism.

Baskakova is radically different from Poliakova. The former shows no interest at all in the struggle for one or another set of principles. Indeed, our author has no love for the Soviet regime—it would be strange to expect anything different from an 80-year-old émigré! Rather, the difference consists in the general aftertaste that her text leaves with the reader. It may be that if Baskakova had been able to complete her memoir and edit it, the result would have been closer to Poliakova's ideas. There are sinister resemblances: both women

---

[63] O. V. Budnitskii and G. S. Zelenina, eds., *"Svershilos'. Prishli nemtsy!": Ideinyi kollaboratsionizm v SSSR v period Velikoi Otechestvennoi voiny* (Moscow: Rossiiskaia politicheskaia entsiklopediia [ROSSPEN], 2012), 27–36. Also available at Stanford University, Hoover Institution Archives. Lidiia Osipov Diary. The banknotes in the publications were identified by Igor Petrov (Munich): https://labas.livejournal.com/tag/осипова.

avoid the darkest episode in the occupation of Pushkin, the extermination of the Jews.[64] Baskakova mentions in passing just one instance, the execution of Doctor Kantsel', and that with strange reservations concerning his bad character. Was Baskakova anti-Semitic? Or is it simply that she saw no need to dwell upon the Holocaust as an obvious fact?

Alternatively, it may be that for Baskakova, as for Poliakova, the decisive factor was that the Holocaust remained an uncomfortable part of history for the Russian émigrés who had "finished up in the West," that is, who had collaborated with the Reich. One of the most horrifying and symbolically loaded episodes in the "Diary of a Collaborator" is a night-time conversation in late June 1944 on the struggle against Bolshevism, on democracy, and on the triumph of good. Through this conversation, Poliakova was trying to distract a young colleague from the sound of gunshots in a nearby cemetery. There, Jews from Riga were being shot, and both women were in an apartment from which Jews had been evicted.[65]

Baskakova and her husband never took part in the "inner emigration," and did not attempt to take their distance from the state. They participated in its activity and defended their interests by legal means, finally resorting to law-breaking only where other methods were impossible. It was this moderation that led them, logically, to emigration—the price of returning to Soviet territory was too high. As "former people," they thus remained "former," but were now former citizens of the USSR. Paradoxically, even pragmatic-minded professionals, people with no history of political involvement and of whom the Soviet regime was in desperate need, remained for it alien, superfluous, and deserving of suspicion.

The city of the poet: At the gates of hell

Twice in the course of the twentieth century, the city of Pushkin, a modern suburb of St. Petersburg and one of its main tourist attractions, finished up on the front lines—during the Russian Civil War and during the Second World War. Pushkin went through the same epidemic of renaming as the former capital of the Russian Empire, Saint Petersburg-Petrograd-Leningrad. After the rev-

---

[64] Pushkin, along with other Leningrad suburbs, can be considered the northern boundary of the zone affected by the Holocaust in the USSR.

[65] Budnitskii and Zelenina, *"Svershilos'. Prishli nemtsy!,"* 175, 176.

olution, the former imperial residence of Tsarskoe Selo became Detskoe Selo ("children's village"), and then, during the turn to the Stalinist "grand style" and "new patriotism," received the name of the symbol of Russian literature. In 1937, the centenary of the poet's death was celebrated in grandiose fashion,[66] and the city was renamed at this time. It may be noted that neighboring Pavlovsk, which after the revolution was renamed Slutsk, got its old name back under the occupiers, and retained it after the war ended.

The former grandeur of Tsarskoe Selo was now placed at the service of the Stalin regime, dressed up in the alien robes of the old empire. The imperial palaces and parks were invoked to symbolize the brilliance of Soviet culture. The place of the Tsarskoe Selo Life Guards in their embroidered uniforms was taken by Red Army units recruited from among workers and peasants, and Pushkin became the site for Command Staff Artillery Courses, AKKUKS. The city was meant to breathe socialist culture: the holiday resort of the Leningrad branch of the Union of Soviet Writers was set up there, and also operating in the city were a laboratory of the Institute of Crop Production, an Agricultural Institute, an Institute of the Milk Industry, seven children's homes, 18 enterprises of various types, and a tuberculosis sanatorium.[67] From 1938, Pushkin was also the site of a home for the children of Spanish republicans, brought as refugees to the USSR.[68] The Spanish connection to Pushkin was to continue. After June 22, 1941, Francoist Spain, formally abstaining from participation in the war against the Soviet Union, had maintained its non-belligerent status. However, the Falangists and radicals of various ilk, passionately wishing to contribute to the "New Order," created a voluntary expeditionary corps which departed to the German-Soviet front. By a cruel irony of fate, this 250th Infantry Division of the Wehrmacht (*División Azul*, the Blue Division), recruited from among Spanish volunteers, was to be quartered in Pushkin during the winter of 1942.[69]

Servicing the museum-preserve and the scientific and medical establishments required educated cadres, and Pushkin was thus home to numerous members of the intelligentsia, including of the old, imperial variety. Among the

---

[66] Jonathan Brooks Platt, *Greetings, Pushkin! Stalinist Cultural Politics and the Russian National Bard* (Pittsburgh, NJ: University of Pittsburgh Press, 2016).

[67] TsGAIPD SPB. F. 2242. Op. 1. D. 441. L. 11. Spiski sekretarei partbiuro, partorgov, rukovodiashchikh rabotnikov g. Pushkin, February 1, 1940.

[68] N. Markov, "My iz Asturii," *Bol'shevistskoe Slovo*, no. 14, April 4, 1938, 2; Karl D. Qualls, *Stalin's Niños: Educating Spanish Civil War Refugee Children in the Soviet Union, 1937–1951* (Toronto: University of Toronto Press, 2020).

[69] Xosé M. Nuñez Seixas, *The Spanish Blue Division on the Eastern Front, 1941–1945: War, Occupation, Memory* (Toronto: University of Toronto Press, 2022).

personnel of the scientific department of the Pushkin palace-museums, four out of 23 people were from noble families and one from a family of the clergy, while ten indicated they were of worker-peasant background.[70] For the earlier-mentioned Ivanov-Razumnik and Khordikainen, who had already suffered repression, Pushkin became a refuge that allowed them to live legally and semi-legally almost in the cultural capital, Leningrad, bypassing the bans that had been imposed on them.

Nevertheless, the conditions of life in the once-elite suburb were far from ideal. As Baskakova was to note, they were far from even being decent. Consumer goods were all in constant short supply; the decrepit housing stock was overcrowded; infrastructure had decayed and was not being replaced; the pathways of once-tidy parks were overgrown; a stream of random people lived for years in the building of the Tsarskoe Selo Lyceum—all these problems figured endlessly in the transcripts of sittings of the Pushkin Regional Soviet and in the pages of the press.[71] There was no way that the gap between the impoverished reality and the ambitions of the eloquent builders of Bolshevism could be concealed. In one of the newspaper feuilletons, Aleksandr Pushkin, the famous Russian poet after whom the city was named, visited the city, and was staggered at the unsightliness of the new way of life.[72]

The prewar period was unclouded only in the propaganda. The Soviet-Finnish War of 1939–1940—the Bolshevik invasion of Finland that ended up in an uneasy peace—effectively resulted in a logistics collapse in Leningrad, with electricity blackouts and shortages of foodstuffs. The moods in Pushkin in 1940, as recorded by the NKVD, were also far from radiant. The Winter War and the annexation of the Baltic states aroused doubts and disquiet. People openly called the ban on independently changing one's job, introduced in 1940, a new serfdom, and the fees for instruction, introduced in the same year, shocked many of the city's teachers and students.[73]

---

[70] TsGAIPD SPB. F. 2242.Op. 1. D. 441. L. 10. Spiski sotrudnikov nauchnogo otdela dvotsov-muzeev g. Pushkin, February 1, 1940–December 31, 1941.

[71] Even the local Soviet newspaper condemned the residents who were destroying housing stock that had once been a cultural treasure. In 1940, there were 62 residential buildings in the city that were in danger of falling into complete ruin. "Khuliganstvuiushchie obitateli dvortsa," *Bol'shevistskoe Slovo*, no. 14, April 4, 1938, 3; TsGA SPB. F. 4958. Op. 1. D. 32. L. 199. "Stenograficheskii otchet zasedaniia 3-i sessii Pushkinskogo raisoveta," July 27, 1940.

[72] A. Beliaev, "Vizit Pushkina: Novogodniaia fantaziia," *Bol'shevistskoe Slovo*, no. 124, January 1, 1939, 3.

[73] TsGAIPD SPB. F. 2242. Op. 1. D. 198. L. 1–7, 23–25, 41–44, 48–55. Spetssvodka RO NKVD o nastroenii naseleniia gor. Pushkin i deiatel'nosti antisovetskogo elementa, January 3, 1940; Spetssoobshchenie, February 16, 1940; Spetssvodka No. 3, April 30, 1940; Spetssvodka, July 2, 1940; Spetssvodka No. 2, 28 June 1940; Spetssvodka, June 26, 1940.

Of course, the events of 1941 overshadowed all the difficulties of peacetime life and completely eclipsed even the revolutionary calamities of 1919. According to German estimates, at the time when the occupation began around 20,000 of Pushkin's 55,000 residents remained in the city.[74] In January 1944, the Soviet forces entered an empty city, reduced to ruins.

The suburbs of Leningrad—Petergof, Strel'na, Gatchina, Pushkin, and Pavlovsk, with all their monuments to the imperial epoch—were among the real victims of the German-Soviet war. The destruction of the palaces and museums was to be one of the charges laid against the German occupiers. In cultural respects, the ruins of the Ekaterininskii Palace in Pushkin and of the Bol'shoi Palace in Petergof became symbols of the blockade tragedy. "Pushkin's city," obliterated by the Nazi barbarians, was described by Ol'ga Berggol'ts and Anna Akhmatova. Even today, the reconstructed Amber Room and the statue of Samson, the originals of which vanished without a trace from Pushkin and Petergof, respectively, have prime places in the list of the most popular objects for curious tourists on their excursions.

A foreign outrage and the victorious rebirth of one of the sacred places of Russian culture have become very important elements in the memory of the blockade. Polina Barskova concludes: "We may imagine that for those who experienced the blockade, the catastrophe of the Ekaterininskii Palace was closely bound up with the catastrophe of Leningrad."[75] In this system, the first and most obvious misconception is the view that "cultural values" overshadow the lives of human beings. The second is that all the destruction and deaths were automatically transformed into crimes of the invaders and that the missing population, including the people who left voluntarily with the Germans, were to be numbered among those who had been "driven off into slavery/captivity," as the Soviet propaganda vaguely put it. The vast crimes of the Germans are well known and are not subject to doubt, but the paradox of the situation in the Leningrad suburbs occupied by them is that most of the shells were fired from the *Soviet* side. The main cause of the destruction was not the evil of the occupiers, but the very fact that military actions were taking place.

A typical example, and one often discussed in the public arena, is the fire in the Ekaterininskii Palace—or, more precisely, in what remained of it—soon after the liberation of the city. There is a version from Soviet times that speaks

---

[74] Jürgen Kilian, *Wehrmacht und Besatzungsherrschaft im Russischen Nordwesten 1941–1944: Praxis und Alltag im Militärverwaltungsgebiet der Heeresgruppe Nord* (Paderborn: Ferdinand Schöningh, 2012), 259.

[75] Barskova, *Sed'maia shcheloch'*, 31.

of delayed-action bombs left by the Wehrmacht, but the reason is likely more prosaic—a careless attitude to fire on the part of the Soviet forces.[76] It is also necessary to mention that the matter was not limited to the bombing and shelling of stations and buildings where important targets were presumed to be located.[77] Applying to Pushkin and other Leningrad suburbs was the notorious Headquarters Order No. 0428 of November 16, 1941 prescribing the comprehensive burning of inhabited points in the immediate German rear. Thus, on November 25, a sabotage group consisting of two youths was sent to Pushkin with instructions to "set fire to as many as 15 wooden buildings." The group, however, was not particularly successful; only one of the saboteurs returned alive and reported that two residential buildings in the suburb had been set alight.[78]

Beyond question, the occupiers plundered single-mindedly, and with respect to the Russian cultural heritage, behaved like vandals. At the same time, recent research on another suburb, Petergof, observes: "Contrary to the established view that the large-scale thefts of artworks were planned in advance and painstakingly organized on a state level, we would like ... to draw special attention to the weakness of the organizational structures, to uncontrolled acts of plunder, and to the competition between separate German agencies."[79] That the occupation regime was not, in essence, a "new order," but rather a "new disorder," seems a very apt observation that encapsulates everything about which Evdokiia Baskakova wrote.

"The little devils of war": The mechanics of violence

In the period from 1941 to 1943, Pushkin was occupied in turn by the SS Police Division, by the 121st Infantry Division, by the 5th Mountain Division, again by the 121st Infantry Division, and by the 250th Infantry, the earlier-mentioned Spanish Blue Division. The city was in the zone of military administration, and representing the regime here were the military commandant's offices or-

---

[76] D. Orlov, "Kto razrushil? Pushkin!," *Gorod (812)*, no. 39 (192), December 11, 2012. https://gorod-812.ru/sovetskie-legendyi-kto-podzhigal-dvortsyi-pushkina-i-petergofa-v-voynu/.

[77] On November 2 and 3, 1941, Soviet aviation bombed the Ekaterininskii Palace in Pushkin and then the Pavlovskii Palace in Pavlov (Slutsk), documenting the explosions. TsAMO RF. F. 217. Op. 1221. D. 189. L. 282, 287, 288. Operativnaia svodka No 125 shtaba VVS Lenfronta, November 2, 1941; Operativnaia svodka No. 127 shtaba VVS Lenfronta, November 3, 1941.

[78] TsGAIPD SPB. F. O-116. Op. 1. D. 816. L. 1–3. Uchetnoe delo diversionnoi gruppy Gumeniuka, November 27, 1941.

[79] *Petergof v Velikoi Otechestvennoi voine: 1941–1945*, vol. 2 (Saint-Petersburg: GMZ "Petergof," 2019), 9.

ganized by the staff of the division that was quartered locally. As Jeff Rutherford points out, there was a paradox on the German side from the beginning: the doctrine of the blitzkrieg required control over the cities as transport hubs and, accordingly, at least their minimum preservation. At the same time, the political goals of the blitzkrieg assumed that Russian cities would be leveled.[80]

In addition, the "temporary order" lasted for more than two years, and the military officers were obliged to maintain contact with the population and to rule over it, which initially they had not anticipated doing. In the broader scheme, the Wehrmacht, by the autumn of 1941, found itself stuck in banal fashion outside Leningrad, by the walls of the city they had not succeeded in capturing. The stake the Germans placed on encirclement and blockade became the first act in the tragedy of the peaceful population of the Leningrad suburbs. The local population simply got in the way of the occupiers, representing an uncontrolled factor in their immediate rear. The army command had no need for the Russian population, and with the exception of Jews and the mentally ill, whom they killed, the Germans were anxious for the population to disappear somewhere of its own accord, and not to obstruct a rethinking of the Wehrmacht's strategic plans.

The simplest solution was to move the civilians outside the zone of military action. In October 1941, the staff of the 18th Army ordered that the available labor force be transported to the rear, singling out Pushkin in particular. But the resources available for carrying this out were insufficient, and by the end of the year, only 32,000 people had been evacuated to distant regions of the province. It will be recalled that approximately 20,000 people remained in Pushkin alone.[81] Here too, it was as though a malevolent fate had divined the wish of the Germans to be rid of the "burden" of the population. By December 1, the staff of the 18th Army had noted that signs of hunger were appearing. Soon the question arose of the extent to which the fighting spirit of the troops would suffer from the fact that women and children were dying of hunger before the soldiers' eyes.[82] In Shlissel'burg, the corps staff, replying to requests from the 1st Infantry Division to have residents evacuated, suggested herding the civilians onto the ice of Lake Ladoga, so as to allow them to go over to the Russians.[83]

---

[80] Jeff Rutherford, *Combat and Genocide on the Eastern Front: The German Infantry's War, 1941–1944* (Cambridge: Cambridge University Press, 2014), 152.

[81] Kilian, *Wehrmacht und Besatzungsherrschaft*, 259.

[82] Kilian, *Wehrmacht und Besatzungsherrschaft*, 282, 283.

[83] NARA. T-314. R. 787. Fr. 813–814. Gen-Kdo XXVII A.K. Ic, Tätigkeitsbericht am 15–16.12.1941.

Almost immediately, the population began dying at an unprecedented rate. During the nightmarish winter of 1941–1942, the situation on the outskirts of Leningrad was almost as bad as within the blockaded city itself. The corpses of animals were used as food, and soon, the corpses being consumed included those of people. Mass deaths among the sick and old became an everyday matter. In Shlissel'burg, it was necessary to create an improvised crematorium to deal with the corpses, just as in Leningrad a crematorium had been set up in a brickworks.[84] Here once again, parallels appear with the epoch of the revolution, since an attempt to introduce the practice of burning bodies had been made for the first time in the city in 1919. At that time, the move had been part of a general offensive against religion and the old way of life, but the outcome had been similar—a temporary structure set up based on industrial furnaces.[85] Pushkin was in a somewhat better position, if that is an acceptable way to put it, since there were more roads leading from the city to the rear. But in the overall scale of the disaster, it differed from the blockaded Leningrad only in the respect that an abundance of abandoned wooden houses solved the problem of obtaining fuel for the ovens.

By the end of the year, the axis of the war had obviously shifted in the direction of a drawn-out conflict. Germans and Russians had somehow to find ways to coexist. From the German point of view, life in the occupation zone for the lower ranks of the Wehrmacht revolved around two elements that were extremely disturbing for the staffs of the 18th Army and Army Group North. These elements, in formal terms strictly forbidden, were barter trade with the locals and contact with women.[86] For Baskakova too, these were prime topics. The barter was at times indistinguishable from looting, and the dealings with women amounted to diverse forms of sexual violence.

Describing this grim everyday world of the occupation, Vera Panova provides us with a strikingly vivid sentence: "It is as though along with the huge black

[84] This was something completely out of the ordinary. The secretary of the city Komsomol, Kirillov, on arriving in the city immediately after its liberation, reported: "I was astonished at the 'crematorium' for burning people's bodies.... There was such a crematorium in a factory settlement ... it had been constructed in an ordinary building." An account by the counter-intelligence department (Ic) of the 227th Infantry Division, captured by Soviet forces in 1943, describes the situation in Shlissel'burg in extremely grim tones. TsGAIPD SPB. F. 4000. Op. 10. D. 7. L. 2 Stenogramma soobshcheniia t.Kirillova Anatoliia Grigor'evicha, sekretaria shlissel'burgskogo gorkoma komsomola, July 5, 1943; TsGA SPB. F. 3355. Op. 18. D. 5. L. 83–89. Spravka nach. 6 otd. Osobogo Otdela 2-i Udarnoi armii, tekst perevedennogo doklada, February 1943.

[85] V. S. Izmozik and N. B. Lebina, *Peterburg sovetskii: "Novyi chelovek" v starom prostranstve; 1920–1930-e gody; sotsial'no–arkhitekturnoe mikroistoricheskoe issledovanie* (Saint-Petersburg: Kriga, 2016), 56–66.

[86] Kilian, *Wehrmacht und Besatzungsherrschaft*, 210.

demon of the war, fearsome little devils are also raging around us, shabby and despicable but also terrifying, especially in their vast number."[87] This was less like the apocalypse than like the time after the apocalypse, as the modern understanding of the genre has it—a new barbarism, a dark epoch amid the fragments of a former world pulverized forever by a global catastrophe.

"Human trash": Normality and deformity

Here we are once again in the "grey zone," in the space that officially does not exist, that should not and cannot exist. As inside Leningrad, along the arc of the encircling front there appeared a strange, inhuman territory. Surviving there would seem to have been impossible, but a great many people nevertheless managed to do it. In this zone, a peculiar system of informal and, strictly speaking, deformed relations became established. Until now, this social system has remained a very painful topic, since everything related to the mechanisms of survival has remained problematic: the social hierarchy, the hierarchy of consumption, concepts of morality (or the lack of it), the frameworks surrounding the exercise of conscience, and the destruction of the human psyche.[88]

Cannibalism is the most flagrant example of this erosion of social norms under conditions when survival is at stake. Unusually, both the occupiers and Leningrad doctors tried initially to explain it in similar fashion. A protocol adopted by a special conference of psychiatrists under the chairmanship of the head of the sanitation department of the Leningrad front declared: "In the majority of cases [cannibalism] is committed by people on a low cultural level, 'human trash'; these are always people marked by low intellect and emotional dullness."[89] The Communications Section of the 121st Infantry Division stated: "These bestial acts in our immediate vicinity have confirmed for us that the rotten beasts are absolutely devoid of feeling, and that when civilians from the circle of the so-called intelligentsia perpetrate this type of act, one cannot expect any better from the subhumans thrown together in the Red Army."[90]

---

[87] Panova, *Moio i tol'ko moio*, 221.

[88] Sergey Yarov, *Leningrad, 1941–1942: Morality in a City under Siege*, transl. Arch Tait (Cambridge: Polity Press, 2017).

[89] TsGSIPD SPB. F. 24. Op. 2b. D. 1383. L. 19. Protokol spetsial'nogo soveshchaniia vrachei-psikhiatrov ekspertov pod predsedatel'stvom nachal'nika sanupravleniia Lenfronta tov. Verkhovskogo, February 23, 1942.

[90] Rutherford, *Combat and Genocide on the Eastern Front*, 186.

Baskakova's text, however, describes only one related case, involving the execution of a woman for having committed cannibalism. To judge from German documents, such things happened, and no one was surprised by them, but they were not commonplace.[91] What was horrifying was that in the "grey zone," it was not obligatory to eat the flesh of thinking beings in order to live at the cost of their demise. Baskakova describes the death of the writer Aleksandr Beliaev; in her words, the family had enough food, but Beliaev's wife left him to starve, giving everything she could obtain to their daughter. Evdokiia formulates, very precisely, an ugly norm, the logic of survival: "It was easy for me to talk and to judge: 'Who is more dear to you, your husband or your child?' Never in my life have I had to face that question."

This is a topic very often encountered in writings from the blockade: "In the family there are children and dependents. People decide who must die. They refrain from feeding these individuals, so that the others can survive."[92] In a deformed world, turned inside out by hunger, the people who in times of peace receive special care finish up low in the hierarchy, while less prestigious work in the kitchen or the graveyard provides a guarantee of well-being. Mutual aid can save people, but it turns readily into support for one's own at the expense of others. One of the heroines of the narrative is an interpreter on the command staff, the Russian-German woman Ol'ga Videman. The "all-powerful Ol'ga Ivanovna" was able to provide help to her daughters and to devote all her efforts to caring for them, but she was completely indifferent to Russian "Untermenschen." The Führer had given his permission to regard the latter as unworthy of life, and so their death meant nothing to her. Meanwhile, the property remaining to random subhumans was simply a resource, to be used for the well-being of one's own family.

This "new (ab)normality" that became established in occupied Pushkin might well be termed "corruption" in the broadest sense of the word. It involved both bribes and informal, mutually advantageous dealings—everything that in the USSR went by the name of *blat*. Also apparent was a general unraveling of social ties, with economic abnormality giving rise to corresponding social and cultural phenomena. Bribery, trade in privileges, and theft were inalienable features of the occupation economy. In the documents, we find the example of

---

[91] In Pavlovsk, in March 1942, four children vanished, and cannibals were suspected. The number of cases recorded in the Pushkin-Pavlovsk region was about five. TsGA SPB F. 9788. Op. 1. D. 7. L. 63. SD Aussenstelle-Pavlovsk, Lage- und Stimmungsbericht 11.3–25.3.1942.

[92] Sergei Iarov, *Blokadnaia etika: Predstavleniia o morali v Leningrade v 1941–1942 gg.* (Moscow: Tsentrpoligraf, 2012), 176–82.

the Pavlovsk burgomaster Gorlin, who in the summer of 1942 was replaced in his post by the Pushkin resident Zolotukhin. Why the substitution? Because Gorlin had been shot by the Nazis for financial machinations and extortion.[93]

Baskakova describes the German commandants and *Sonderführer* hunting both for booty and simply for adequate food; she also depicts the black market and the system of informal patron-client ties. In this strange world, where people behaved toward one another like wolves, personal ties were the umbilical cord that permitted survival. The importance of these bonds was difficult to exaggerate. Ultimately, it was thanks to such ties that the evacuation to Germany of Baskakova herself and her family was possible.

Similar phenomena are noted in a study by James Heinzen devoted to corruption in the postwar Stalinist USSR. The author concludes that the war played a decisive role in the formation of this system.[94] It would be a worthy undertaking to draw parallels with what happened in the occupied territories, though this topic, like the occupation economy as a whole, requires a separate monograph. However huge the difference between the Nazi occupation of Central and Western Europe and the Soviet territories had been—and indeed, it was huge—the same image of occupation, characterized by social chaos and corruption, emerges in some academic accounts. Tony Judt perceives the occupation as "the utter collapse of law and the habits of life in a legal state. To live normally in occupied Europe meant breaking the law: in the first place the laws of the occupiers ... but also conventional laws and norms as well.... Violence became part of daily life.... Violence bred cynicism."[95]

Thus, a peculiarity of the occupation zone, it would seem, was that corruption did not serve merely as the "grease" that kept the crude mechanisms of the mobilization economy functioning. In essence, *all* daily life played itself out in the empty spaces between the policies of the various Reich departments, and everything was *provisional*. Leningrad never fell, and so long as the Reich hierarchs occupied themselves with projects for exploiting the territories that had been seized, the population that had been left out of account in these projects could rely only on informal methods to survive. Even for people who collaborated with the Nazis, that is, for "privileged" individuals such as the Baskakov-Bogachev couple, the path was one of hardship and humiliation.

---

[93] TsGA SPB. F. 9788. Op. 1. D. 11. L. 49, Einsatzgruppe A, Lagebericht am 15.6.1942; F. 3355 Op. 10. D. 271. L. 166. *Politseiskie Vedomosti (Pavlovsk)*, no. 4, June 6, 1942, 4.

[94] Heinzen, *The Art of the Bribe.*

[95] Tony Judt, *Postwar: A History of Europe since 1945* (New York: The Penguin Press, 2005), 36–37.

An (un)sentimental war: The image of womanhood

According to German data, in 1943 women made up 60 percent of the population of the occupied territories. Without a doubt, the history of the occupation
was above all female, as is evident from the sources already cited, and if one
examines the contemporary interviews in the genre of oral history that were
collected in Leningrad Province, the respondents were indeed mostly women.[96]

In general, the ideal Soviet man or woman was supposed to exist on a higher
human plane where questions of gender no longer figured. The new role of
people in "advanced" society endowed them with the kind of wings that allowed them to soar above such matters that were now viewed as happily settled. Where the female share in the history of the blockade is concerned, the
theme of "women in the fight for the city of Lenin" was present from the very
beginning. Meanwhile, women in this narrative were reduced to the status of
passive victims, calling others to action (or to vengeance), or who, alternatively,
were "manly young women" (the citation here is quite literal).[97]

Real life, however, differed strikingly from the ideal. The land of the Soviets was an unusual expanse, where seemingly progressive goals were pur-
sued using the most backward, primitive, and at times also cruel methods—
a mix of compulsion, violence, pumped-up campaigns, and necessity. Before
the war as well, the Bolshevized society had combined a declarative champi-
oning of women's emancipation with the crudest gender conservatism at the
grassroots level.[98]

With the coming of war, the social relations that had been maintained, if
barely, through public campaigns and the enthusiasm of the "new men and
women" regressed to their old, archaic level. At the same time, the state was
faced with an acute need for rapid and universal mobilization. The pieces of
a mosaic made up of gender relations, scraps of prewar policies, propagandist
diatribes, "new norms," and wartime pragmatism were assembled into a varie-
gated jigsaw puzzle. Glistening on its surface was the bravery of women snipers,
along with young collective Liudmila Pavlichenkos and the all-female 588th
Night Bomber Regiment. The lower levels featured sordid stories of the dissi-

---

[96] For example, 25 of the 34 interviews in Aleksei Vinogradov and Albert Jan Pleysier, *Okkupatsiia
Leningradskoi oblasti v gody Velikoi Otechestvennoi Voiny* (Saint-Petersburg: Izdatel'stvo "LEMA,"
2006).

[97] Antonina A. Nikiforova, *Povest' o bor'be i druzhbe* (Leningrad: Lenizdat, 1967), 117.

[98] On the prewar gender situation, see Natalia Lebina, *Sovetskaia povsednevnost': normy i anomalii; Ot
voennogo kommunizma k bol'shomu stiliu* (Moscow: Novoe Literaturnoe Obozrenie, 2016), 224–69.

pation of officers with "campaign-field wives" and harems of well-groomed telephonists in the staff offices, against a background composed of a downtrodden, hungry rank and file.

Curiously, the situation with these ill-assorted memories has been preserved for the most part to this day. The Soviet stereotypes jostle against the real histories of female soldiers, with eyewitness testimonies that speak of extreme discomfort.[99] Even more complex are the stories of civilian women during the war, stories that cannot be reduced to accounts of military successes and of the number of enemies shot.

Where the occupation as a whole was concerned, all the suffering and conflict caused by the war were only permitted to be linked to the enemy. A language for describing the trauma thus came into being, a language that at the same time determined how the history of the war was to be written. The life of a woman under the Germans was depicted in terms of a dichotomy: either as unrelieved suffering, a hell from the point of view of her soul that languished within it, or as a struggle against the forces of darkness in the enemy's lair. The question of collaboration with the Germans was posed in just as unequivocal a fashion, as a choice between two alternatives: either waging a struggle against them or engaging in outright treachery. To view the day-to-day survival of city residents in terms of these categories was simply impossible, and these considerations were thus banished to a "grey zone" that was not supposed to exist. In terms of style, this was logical: the struggle to gain access to the food scraps from the soldiers' kitchen, or the intrigues surrounding the acquisition of an entry pass to a restricted area, were in no way suitable as subjects for high tragedy.

A "mission for the skilled": Women under the occupation

All the bizarre distortions of the theme of women during the greatest war in the history of the USSR are echoed in the blockade tragedy. Thus, in Leningrad an analogue existed to the "campaign-field wives"—the "blockade wives,"

---

[99] Artiom Drabkin and Bair Irincheev, eds., *"A zori zdes' gromkie": Zhenskoe litso voiny* (Moscow: Iauza, 2012). In this collection of interviews, women veterans mention the contemptuous attitudes shown toward them, the harassment they were subjected to in the army, and even attempts at rape. The contradictions involved in the topic are obviously painful. In a 2017 collection of women's recollections entitled *Sestry po oruzhiiu* (Sisters in arms), the aim of the book is described as being "to stress the achievements ... and to dispel the harmful myths that have filled the press in recent years." Bair Irincheev, Mikhail Zinov'ev, Viacheslav Davydkin et al., eds., *Sestry po oruzhiiu: Vospominaniia o Velikoi Otechestvennoi voine* (Vyborg: Izdatel'stvo "Voenno-istoricheskii tsentr peresheika," 2016–2017), 7, 8.

that is, women in the starving city who cohabited with high-status men or who simply procured food through sex.[100] In the suburbs of Leningrad, just as inside the ring of the blockade, gender roles and hierarchies were shattered.[101] First, there were simply greater numbers of women. Large numbers of men of working age had been conscripted into the Red Army. All those who held significant posts sought to leave, and in the initial period after the Germans arrived, all males aged from 14 to 55 were subject to confinement in labor camps.[102]

Medicine, to which Evdokiia Baskakova devoted herself, had become a very highly valued pursuit in the conditions of catastrophe. Within the profession, the position of women had traditionally been strong, and Baskakova, in her text, recalls a large number of female colleagues. It is known that the hospital for civilians in Pushkin was headed by Zinaida Kabardova,[103] and that working as a sanitary physician in neighboring Pavlovsk was a woman named Annenkova.[104] Work in the knitwear factory, which gave the right to a ration and a wage, required skills in knitting and sewing, traditional women's pursuits.

Such was the position in the official sphere that was regulated by the occupiers and in which Baskakova and her husband had been able to obtain employment. However, most of the population found themselves in the unofficial sphere, trying to fend for themselves. From being a routine and mildly despised "job for the weak," housework—washing clothes, cleaning, buying and preparing food—was transformed into a "mission for the skilled," into risk-laden day-to-day operations on which people's very survival depended. In

---

[100] Alexis Peri, *The War Within: Diaries from the Siege of Leningrad* (Harvard, MA: Harvard University Press, 2017), 145–47. Cohabitation with women subordinates and waitresses figures in the compromising materials gathered by the NKVD on generals Feofan Lagunov, Filipp Kriukov, Mikhail Khozin, and Filipp Rybal'chenko: TsGAIPD SPB. F. 24. Op. 2b. D. 1323. L. 16–23. Soobshchenie nachal'nika Osobogo Otdela NKVD Leningradskogo fronta Kuprina sekretariu Len. Obkoma VKP(b) A. A. Zhdanovu, January 17, 1942; Spravka po dokladu starshego operupolnomochennogo t. Shustorovicha i operupolnomochennogo leitenanta GB t. Komarova, 6 marta 1942; Agenturnoe donesenie istochnika "Sokolova," March 1942.

[101] Hass, *Wartime Suffering and Survival*, 135–79.

[102] Johannes Hürter, "Die Wehrmacht vor Leningrad: Krieg und Besatzungspolitik der 18. Armee im Herbst und Winter 1941/42," *Vierteljahrshefte für Zeitgeschichte* 49, no. 3 (2001): 411.

[103] In 1944, Kabardova was evacuated by the Germans to Windau (now Ventspils). TsGA SPB. F. 8557. Op. 6. D. 1095. L. 22. Protokol doprosa Krylova Sergeia Vasil'evicha, February 13, 1944; NARA. T-311. R. 115. Fr. 7154713. Verzeichnis der von der Aussenstelle der Abt.VII (O.Q.Nord) erfassten Angehörigen der ehem. Russ. landeseigenen Verwaltung, die sich zum Arbeitsansatz in Deutschland eignen, Stand 1 Juni 1944.

[104] We have virtually no information concerning the Pushkin hospital. Documents from the hospital in Pavlovsk have been preserved, and disease histories studied by the authors put the ratio of recoveries to deaths in the winter of 1942 at 17:2. The causes of death were wounds, pneumonia, and exhaustion. TsGA SPB. F. 3355. Op. 10. D. 265. L. 1–60. History of the illnesses of the patients of Pavlovsk hospital for civilians, September–December 1941; F. 3355. Op. 10. D. 271. L. 170, 173. *Politseiskie Vedomosti (Pavlovsk)*, no. 6, July 1, 1942, 1 and no. 7, July 10, 1942, 2.

Pushkin, ration cards for bread were introduced only in the summer of 1942, meaning that until then, survival was the responsibility of the starving individuals themselves. For those in the city who lacked an income and a source of supply, "women's work" was the sole means of staying fed. Washing and mending clothes, cleaning premises, and performing kitchen tasks—the occupiers needed these services on a daily basis, and were prepared to pay for them with food. Such precious goods as kerosine, matches, and salt could be "organized" only through barter, and the Germans were the monopolists and sole source of these commodities.[105]

Once again, we are talking of a "grey zone" in which one of the sides in the contacts was in a dependent situation, even one of enslavement in the literal sense. Often, this situation involved sexual coercion. It is true that there were degrees of this coercion; not all the liaisons led in a straightforward fashion to sexual slavery, since there existed both voluntary relationships[106] and "soft" economic compulsion.[107] Official soldiers' brothels operated, where local women went to work voluntarily, if that is the appropriate word.[108] Nevertheless, what is most striking is the arbitrary, indiscriminate violence against women.

Evdokiia Baskakova describes a whole epidemic of rape. The same cases are recalled by witnesses who provided statements to the Soviet commission that investigated crimes by the occupiers. In the Khordikainen family, thirteen-year-old Sofiia (Zosia), the sister of Liusia Khordikainen, became a rape victim.[109] Baskakova's detailed description of the murder of Elena Matskevich matches the declaration prepared for a Soviet commission by Elena's stepfather.[110]

---

[105] Partisans reported that this situation existed even in such provinces, distant from the front and suffering relatively lightly, as Novgorod (Shimsk and Porkhovsk regions): "The population are obliged to obtain kerosine and matches from German soldiers in exchange for agricultural products." TsGAIPD SPB. F. O-116. Op. 9. D. 254. L. 29. Report by the head of the Novgorod inter-regional underground center Beliaev, December 1942.

[106] Baskakova recalls the Neverovskii family, who left with the Spaniards of the Blue Division. It is known that in Pavlovsk in April 1942 a German soldier submitted a request to be married to a local woman. Kilian, *Wehrmacht und Besatzungsherrschaft*, 210.

[107] Seventeen-year-old Marusia, living in Shlissel'burg, describes the position of her friend Nelia in this fashion: "Neumann said, either live with him or go. Giving in to him meant having all her needs met, but no longer being a virgin, while not giving in meant losing her last piece of bread." TsGA SPB. F. 3351. Op. 16. D. 31. L. 9. Diary of the girl Marusia (extracts), entry from March 27, 1942.

[108] In Pavlovsk in early March 1942, the SD conducted checks on six women who sought to work in the brothel of the 121st Infantry Division: TsGA SPB. F. 9788. Op. 1. D.9. L. 2. Sicherheitspolizei und SD Aussenstelle Pawlowsk, Tätigkeitsbericht 23.02.–12.03.1942.

[109] Nuridzhanova, *Zhizn' v okkupatsii i pervye poslevoennye gody*, 23, 24.

[110] TsGA SPB. F. 4557. Op. 6. D. 1095. L. 97. Zaiavlenie Odintsova Leonida Mikhailovicha v Komissiiu po rassledovaniiu zverstv nemetsko-fashistskikh band i ustanovleniiu nanesennogo imi ushcherba, February 24, 1944.

Matskevich worked for a German unit and was loyal to the occupiers; in Baskakova's words, she even changed the thinking of Germans who nourished sympathies for Soviet socialism.

Like the attempt, mentioned by Baskakova, to rape the daughter of the interpreter Videman, the commandant's key assistant, this case shows that the occupation was a strange inhuman space without clear guarantees. Even if anarchy did not prevail there, the rule by the German authorities was inconsistent and often weak, and the gaps in the competence of the occupation regime were filled by chaotic savagery. No one could be sure, even in areas of formal work, who would be "at the wheel" the following day. Relations established with the personnel of one regiment were of no help if one encountered soldiers of a different unit. Bombs fell all about, including those dropped by people formally on one's own side. The only guarantee of safety was to be under constant protection, but this was something that almost no one possessed. All shared activity was constructed on the basis of slender personal ties, and these might be severed at any moment.

In her "diary of a collaborator," Poliakova recalls events around New Year 1942. "In the city, one effort at amusement ended tragically. The Germans were with their 'girlfriends.' The officers got drunk and began mocking the women. The latter defended themselves, and during a fight a lamp fell over and the building caught fire. The women rushed to escape, but the officers began hunting after them as if they were rabbits. Three of the women were killed, and another injured."[111] A similar case is noted in documents of the German security service (SD, *Sicherheitsdienst*) in Pavlovsk. On the night of March 8, 1942, a visit by a lance-corporal to the house of a young woman he knew ended with the murder of her father, a chase after the woman herself, and the rape of another woman. To judge from the testimonies, the victims had been engaged in discreet prostitution with soldiers.[112] The case provoked a scandal and led to an investigation, but in practice the army staff were only worried by the prospect that the violence might affect the fighting capacity of the forces. A constant headache for the command was venereal diseases. In March 1942, a sanitary company of the 121st Infantry Division identified 16 infected women. Following treatment, they were marked out by being made to wear white armbands, after which rumors circulated that the Germans were branding infected women

---

[111] Budnitskii and Zelenina, *"Svershilos'. Prishli nemtsy!,"* 113.

[112] TsGA SPB. F. 9788. Op. 1. D. 44. L. 96–106. Stabskompanie Inf.-Regt. 407, der SS-Sicherheitspolizei, March 8, 1942; Sicherheitspolizei und SD Aussenstelle Pawlowsk, Niederschrift, March 9, March 10, March 12, 1942.

on the cheek.[113] The nature of the rumors shows precisely how the local residents perceived their situation.

Jürgen Kilian has already noted how the principle of unquestioning submission in the Wehrmacht turned into complete impunity with regard to civilians.[114] Baskakova, reflecting on the difference between the Germans and the Spanish, describes this paradoxical connection as follows: "The Spanish soldier is just as much a rapist as the German, with the sole difference that if the woman or girl puts up the slightest resistance, he leaves her be, without doing anything to her, while the German soldier is a one-hundred-percent rapist. Once he has seized his victim, he never lets her out of his hands, and afterwards—afterwards he shoots her. This is explained by the fact that the German soldier is subject to strict discipline and answers to a military court. The Spanish army is very lax, and the soldiers are not afraid of their commanders."

The idea that the Spanish legionaries of the 250th Division of the Wehrmacht were distinguished by their disorderliness and "lax morals" has long been commonplace, and is part of the legend of the "benevolent occupiers" that veterans of the Blue Division sought to cultivate. The impulsiveness, sentimentality, and sexual ardor of the "hot-blooded Iberians" is indeed noted in all the sources the present authors have studied, and not least in the diary of Poliakova. In practice, however, this Spanish "zest for life" turned into the same crimes, only with a different shade of the theatrically absurd.[115] Vladimir Kovalevskii, a Russian émigré and interpreter who served with the Blue Division in 1941 even before its transfer to Pushkin, described in his memoirs the same endemic thievery and sexual violence, the latter both overt and in the disguised form of forced cohabitation.[116] If we are to believe Kovalevskii, the staff of the Blue Division was surrounded by a whole host of young Russian women, exchanging their bodies for safety and nutrition.[117]

---

[113] TsGA SPB. F. 9788. Op. 1. D. 7. L. 67. SD Aussenstelle-Pawlowsk, Lage- und Stimmungsbericht, 11.3–25.3.1942.

[114] Kilian, *Wehrmacht und Besatzungsherrschaft*, 55–60.

[115] Xosé M. Núñez Seixas, "Good Invaders? The Occupation Policy of the Spanish Blue Division in Northwestern Russia, 1941-1944," *War in History* 25, no. 3 (2018): 361–86; Xosé M. Núñez Seixas, "Russia and the Russians in the Eyes of the Spanish Blue Division Soldiers, 1941-4," *Journal of Contemporary History* 52, no. 2 (2017): 352–74.

[116] On Russians in Spain, see Xosé M. Núñez Seixas and Oleg Beyda, "'Defeat, Victory, Repeat': Russian Émigrés between the Spanish Civil War and Operation Barbarossa, 1936-1944," *Contemporary European History* (2023): 1–16, https://doi.org/10.1017/S0960777323000085.

[117] Xosé M. Núñez Seixas and Oleg Beyda, eds., *An Anti-Communist on the Eastern Front: The Memoirs of a Russian Officer in the Spanish Blue Division (1941-1942)* (Yorkshire–Philadelphia: Pen & Sword Books Ltd, 2023), 146–48; originally published in Russian in Oleg Beyda and Xosé M. Núñez Seixas, eds., *Ispanskaia grust': Golubaia diviziia i pokhod v Rossiu, 1941-1942 gg.: vospominaniia V. I. Kovalevskogo* (Moscow, Saint-Petersburg: Nestor-Istoriia, 2021), 128–30.

Although Kovalevskii was a lover of hyperbole and heightened colors, his remarks take on a different tone if we compare them with Baskakova's text and with other sources. A cross-comparison allows one to state that within the framework of the corrupt occupation economy there existed (apart from the official brothels) a whole market in female sexual services. In availing themselves of it, the Spaniards differed little from the Germans, exploiting in predatory fashion the difficult position in which women found themselves. A direct consequence of this "black coital economy" was a clandestine market for abortions. The physician Elena Matskevich, who was to be murdered in the course of an attempted rape, was herself an abortion provider. One cannot help noting that Baskakova describes a situation that, in the way it developed (not in its culmination, that is, Matskevich's death), was prefigured by the reality of the Soviet Union in the prewar period. In the USSR, the legislation relating to abortion changed several times to its direct opposite. Contraception remained effectively inaccessible. Despite strict bans, abortions were performed everywhere. Those who had connections and money could have the operation performed by a physician on a private basis, but for women who lacked those advantages, the only resort was a dangerous, excruciatingly painful self-abortion.[118]

Formally speaking, the staff of the 18th Army forbade military servicemen even such things as walking arm-in-arm with a Russian woman, along with dancing and the exchanging of photographs.[119] In practice, the lower ranks of the Wehrmacht could commit *any* act of violence, so long as it did not leave obvious traces. Officers could permit themselves not just "concubines," but even, if they wished, the illusion of a family home. Baskakova describes something like "salons" hosted by the interpreter Videman and the Neverovskii family; she stresses that these "did not always have a sexual sub-plot," though local residents considered that Videman was "trading" in her young daughters. Most likely, evenings spent with music and in the company of women actually were, in the first instance, a means of relaxing and finding distraction from the routines of the war, or even of feeling oneself capable of empathy.

Such a "deficit of feelings" could also be observed among the people of the occupied zone, and notably among the "girlfriends of the Germans," as Poliakova describes them. We have already cited the diary left by the 17-year-old Marusia from Shlissel'burg; in it, she reveals her yearning for personal relationships and seeks romance, while also recognizing that with the German

---

[118] Lebina, *Sovetskaia povsednevnost'*, 246–69.

[119] TsGA SPB. F. 9788. Op. 1. D. 59. L. 95. Order Armee-Oberkommando 18 Nr. 602/42, April 20, 1942.

soldiers who caught her eye, no such relationships would happen.[120] The same may be seen in the writings of 16-year-old Mariia Kuznetsova, living in Staraia Russa. Her story is profoundly tragic. Her diary, with its jottings about dances with German beaus and its curses directed at the two tyrants who had engineered the worldwide slaughter, was to consign her to a Soviet prison camp, where she died of pellagra.[121]

The harassment of women who had engaged in amorous relations with occupiers has an international history. The "concubines" of German soldiers were subjected to persecution almost everywhere, from Denmark, through all of Europe, to Serbia.[122] The "salons" of Ol'ga Videman would have been quite likely to result in her being shot. Thus, near Luga between January 15–17, 1944, a "troika" of the 11th Partisan Brigade sentenced to death four women who had been charged with "maintaining a den for German officers," with denouncing people, with working as an interpreter, with consorting with Germans, and with "prostitution involving German officers."[123] In the USSR, of course, "sexual collaborationism" was seen as an outrage from all points of view, from the popular-cynical angle as well as from the official-heroic one. Sex itself was a dubious topic; in the public arena and in literature, even a hint of sexuality was cause for accusations of "physiologism," "unnecessary naturalness," and so forth.[124] Further, in the USSR the degree of "permitted" contact with the occupiers was vanishingly small. The very fact of having been in occupied territory or of having performed forced labor for the Germans persisted as a stain on one's biography that was impossible to remove. An entry on a personal file could at any moment act as a time bomb, so to have such a past was something that one was, decidedly, better off without.

Citizens who knew the nature of the Bolshevik regime and who had remained "under the Germans" had no illusions about the effect of this on their prospects.

---

[120] TsGA SPB. F. 3355. Op. 16. D. 31. L. 2–10. Diary of the girl Marusia (extracts), February 11–April 16, 1942.

[121] Electronic publication on the "Prozhito" site: https://prozhito.org/notes?date=%221941-01-01%22&diaries=%5B1259%5D.

[122] Anette Warring, *Tyskerpiger Under Besœttelse og Retsopgør* (Copenhagen: Gyldendal, 2017); Ljubinka Škodrić, "Intimate Relations between Women and the German Occupiers in Serbia 1941–1944," *Cahiers balkaniques*, no. 43 (2015), http://journals.openedition.org/ceb/8589.

[123] TsGAIPD SPB. F. O-116. Op. 1. D. 2240. L. 15–18. Resheniia partizanskogo suda 11-i Volkhovskoi partizanskoi brigady ot 15 ianvaria i 17 ianvaria 1944.

[124] This argument was used against the Leningrad writer Evgenii Fedorov, who in 1944 published a novel about partisans in Leningrad Province. He was not permitted to stake a claim to such a potentially lucrative topic, see M. V. Zolotonosov, *Gadiushnik: Leningradskaia pisatel'skaia organizatsiia; izbrannye stenogrammu s kommentariiami; Iz istorii sovetskogo literaturnogo byta 1940–1960-kh godov* (Moscow: Novoe Literaturnoe Obozrenie, 2013), 128–29.

For example, the physician Petrov from the settlement of Sablino, twenty kilometers from Pushkin, left a diary in which he wrote in November 1943 that he would find it easier to "sit out 5–10 years in a concentration camp in Soviet Russia than to wander about foreign countries."[125] Even work in a relatively peaceful job, with no direct link to helping the occupiers, seemed to Petrov to be an infraction for which retribution would necessarily come. There is no doubt that the Baskakov-Bogachev family saw their position in the same terms of "crime and punishment." This was entirely reasonable, since even the most favorable outcome for them would involve many years in remote exile. In addition, we do not know how far the couple's collaboration with the Wehrmacht extended. This story will probably never be told in full.

For many years, a past that included life under the occupation—like the past for many people who have suffered from violence—was not something that could be accepted impassively. It was either grounds for accusations or something about which to remain silent. The awkwardness of Baskakova's memoir is valuable precisely because it helps us give events back their autonomy. As can be seen, the history of Baskakova and the histories of those she remembers are of little use as didactic examples. We are left with an uncomfortable conclusion: in each case, the motives of the collaborators were different, and the evaluations that must be made of their behavior are different as well. Almost every member of Soviet society possessed traits that might at any moment have caused them to be declared a marginal element, and a cocktail of resentments, fear, and a habit of adapting provided a common background for the "people under the Germans" (that is, people who worked for the occupiers). But how far a person might go under the influence of this background depended on their own character and motives, and their participation in Nazi crimes bore little relation to the harm they had suffered from the prewar Stalinist terror.

The tank armadas and the squadrons of aircraft filling the skies have stayed in the past, but "displaced persons," blockaded cities, and peaceful civilians forced to drag out an unimaginable existence between the positions of warring sides remain depressingly familiar. In the same way, the Second World War, at once contemporary and hopelessly remote, is similar in the depth and inexorability of the human suffering it witnessed, even though its trappings were quite different.

---

[125] TsGA SPB. F. 3355. Op. 13. D. 16. L. 30. Diary of E. P. Petrov, physician at the Sablino polyclinic, entry from November 7, 1943.

One thing is certain: with respect to civilian populations, all wars are the same, and most of their unwilling participants will always remain "superfluous" and "unnecessary" in the discourse of the new human slaughter. Evdokiia Baskakova began, but never completed, this account by a woman civilian, a story "from the sidelines of war." Nevertheless, she lived a long and, it seems, productive life. Her writings are a memorial to those who did not succeed in living out their lives. When we recall the nightmare that unfolded around her, the degradation of human nature and the bacchanalia of unrestricted violence, we can say with confidence that she and her husband were "fortunate."

Perhaps even without the inverted commas.

The recollections of
Evdokiia Vasil'evna Baskakova-Bogacheva

Here are the recollections of E[vdokiia] V[asil'evna] Bogacheva-Baskakova.[1]

Benda Street. Merryland. 2160
Australia N.S.W
in reply to a letter from
Mr. Secretary A[ndrei] Naidenov
of March 28, 1970.[2]

After reading the article "A Dignified Old Age" by Pavel Perov, which appeared
in the Sunday issue of N[ovoe] R[usskoe Slovo] on February 9, 1969,[3] I decided
that, having lived such a long life (81 years), I should present for judgment my
curriculum vitae and share with the author my life's experience. I must warn
the author that I am not from the first wave of emigration but from the second,
having arrived in Australia in 1951. I myself, E[vdokiia] V[asil'evna] B[askakova],
was born in Moscow on February 29, 1888, so that as a "leap year baby" I can
claim to be only 20 years old. My husband, V[ladimir] M[ikhailovich] B[ogachev],

---

[1] Although technically, her maiden family name (Baskakova) should come first and her husband's
family name (Bogacheva) second, this order was in some cases, like here, reversed.

[2] According to journal no. 6 for the recording of all materials received by the Museum of Russian
Culture in San Francisco, the manuscript arrived on June 6, 1970, and was forwarded for stor-
age to the archive department. Naidenov's letter of March 1970 has not been preserved.

[3] Pavel Perov (1888–1980) was a journalist and writer, and a member of the editorial board of *Novoe
Russkoe Slovo* (New Russian Word). In the article he called for writing down and preserving the memories of émigrés as part of the history of Russia: "Every émigré is a part of the 'slice' that has been
cut off from the body of the homeland, and it is up to him or her to ensure that this 'slice' does not
wither, that it does not cease to exist, but that it enters as a living element into the Russian history
of the twentieth century." *Novoe Russkoe Slovo*, no. 20425, February 8, 1969, 2. On Perov's devious
and at times dubious biography, see L. S. Fleishman, "Iz istorii zhurnalistiki russkogo zarubezh'a: k
biografii V. M. Despotuli (po pis'mam ego k. G. Kromiadi)," in *Istoriia literatury; Poetika; Kino: Sbornik v chest' Marietty Omarovny Chudakovoi* (Moscow: Novoe izdatel'stvo, 2013), 371–449.

was born in Kiev in 1886, and received his education first in Moscow and then in St. Petersburg, where he completed his studies at the 1st Gymnasium,[4] and then at the Faculty of Law of the University.[5] He was not awarded a diploma, since he was not admitted to the state examinations for refusing to sit for the preliminary examination in theology.

Early Life[6]

In my case, I completed my studies at the 3rd Moscow Gymnasium[7] and moved to St. Petersburg in order to enter the W[omen's] M[edical] I[nstitute]. I wanted very much to practice medicine. Living in St. Petersburg was my older sister, who was married to the older brother of my husband, and this was also one of the reasons why I went to study in SPb. My relatives, and especially my sister-in-law, the wife of my brother, promised to help me and to pay my tuition fees at the institute. This sister-in-law was at that time completing dentistry courses in Moscow and seemed envious of the fact that I was to study medicine.[8]

In those days, the title of dentist did not carry a great deal of weight. But she must be given her due—she became a very good dentist, and her home clientele included even high-placed figures from the Kremlin. This proved very advantageous to her during the Yezhov period,[9] when her husband, my brother Al[eksan]dr Vas[il'evi]ch, was arrested. As his wife, she rushed to her influential patients and was able to ensure that his sentence was limited to exile at a distance of at least 100 km [62 miles] from Moscow. My brother had always said that he would work (he was an agent arranging the sale of paper from Finnish factories) only until he was 50 and would then be a "free bird." He was a wonderful sportsman, a cross-country skier who also took part in boating—he

---

4   The personal file of the pupil of the 1st Gymnasium, Vladimir Bogachev, for 1901–1906 is held in the archive, but is in an unsatisfactory state and is not accessible. TsGIA SPB. F. 114. Op. 1. D. 9279.

5   He was a student from 1906 until 1913. TsGIA SPB. F. 14. Op. 3. D. 45642. L. 14. Lichnoe delo studenta Vladimira Mikhailovicha Bogacheva.

6   These section headings have been introduced by the editors of the current volume for clarity and the reader's navigation.

7   The 3rd Women's Gymnasium was one of six gymnasiums for girls under the Department of the Empress Mariia. It was located on Ulitsa Bol'shaia Ordynka. P. N. Ariian, *Pervyi zhenskii kalendar' na 1900 g.* (Saint-Petersburg: Tovarishchestvo pechati i izdatel'skogo dela "Trud," 1900), 143.

8   Anastasiia Pavlovna Baskakova, dentist, and Aleksandr Vasil'evich Baskakov are shown in a 1914 Moscow address book as living at 6 Pereulok Stolesnikov. *Vsia Moskva: Adresnaia i spravochnaia kniga na 1914 g.* (Moscow: Izdatel'stvo A. S. Suvorina "Novoe Vremia," 1914), 900.

9   The reference is to the Great Terror of 1937–1938.

sailed gigs in a yacht club—and he preferred to have an apartment not in Moscow but in its suburbs. For many years, he lived in Kuskovo in the former orangeries of the Sheremet'evskii Palace, which had been remodeled and let out.[10]

After receiving the order to leave, he set out along the Riazan' railway line to Bykovo station, to his former game warden, and spent many years living in the forest. He pitched a tent and obtained necessities with the help of his wife and children—he had two children, a son, Andrei, and a daughter, Tania.[11] They all visited him since they were themselves exceptional at sporting activities. Andrei, after graduating from a technical institute, was sent to America-Mexico. When he went there, he learned dances, the foxtrot, and in Moscow he went looking for headwear, a fedora.

He was unable to find a hat and bought one in Germany. He learned the foxtrot on a ship. From America, he brought back a motorcycle. He rode about on it with his wife, Lidochka Bogacheva, his cousin, the daughter of the elder Bogachev, Nikolai. Nikolai was married to my older sister, Lidiia Baskakova, while I, the younger Baskakova, Evdokiia, was married to the younger Bogachev, Vladimir.[12] In Moscow, people feasted their eyes on the motorcycle, and when it was parked, a crowd would gather around it. I don't know if he knew the reason why he was arrested, and my husband and I found out about it only here, when we read a book of reminiscences by Prof[essor] Ignat'ev, where he mentions General Baskakov, who had taught a course on tactics at the Military Academy.[13] Earlier, there were rumors that my brother had been taken for a military big shot, when of course he could prove that he had performed normal military service as a cadet, going on from secondary school to officer training. His wife's dental practice helped her gain access to her high-placed patients, and to show that her husband had had nothing to do with generals.

Meanwhile, I had enrolled in the Women's Medical Institute, and despite being only a student in the fourth course, made use of my knowledge of surgical practice, performing an operation on my husband to cut the Achilles tendon of his right foot, of course, not through its whole thickness. This was done to secure his full exemption from military service.

---

[10] Kuskovo, the estate of the counts Sheremet'ev, is now part of Moscow.

[11] On Andrei Aleksandrovich Baskakov and Tatiana Aleksandrovna Baskakova, no information could be found.

[12] Similarly, searches for information on Lidiia Baskakova and Nikolai Bogachev yielded no results.

[13] "The grim Colonel Baskakov, who menaced us at examinations and in practical exercises." Baskakova mistakenly identifies Count Ignatiev as a professor. A. A. Ignatiev, *Piat'desiat let v stroiu*, vol. 1 (Moscow: Voenizdat, 1986), 97.

My husband, Vladimir Mikhailovich Bogachev, was a follower of L[ev] N[ikolaevich] Tolstoi on questions of Christian religion and belief, as was I. We married when we were students, simply walking out of the house of his parents, where I rented a room. All this left the Bogachev family very upset, especially my husband's second-oldest brother, Georgii Mikhailovich Bogachev, a colonel of the 2nd Artillery Brigade of the Life Guards.[14]

This was in about 1911. Georgii tried at length to persuade us, and in the end, we agreed to stand beneath our crowns in a church while he would set everything up and obtain the papers for the church announcement, confession, communion, and the other things needed for the wedding. The ceremony took place in the village of Sablino in the Tosnenskii region, where the Bogachevs had a dacha.[15] Ten years later, this very same church saw the christening of my son Vladimir,[16] with whom I had to provide myself [sic.] in order to save myself from being drafted for military service during the Civil War.[17] Earlier, we had taken the view that both children and parents were evils, with the only difference being that children were an avoidable evil, while parents were an unavoidable one.

Chaos: The First World War, the Civil War, and the early years of Soviet power

I was placed at the disposal of the Southwestern Front and to obtain a referral travelled to Smolensk, since there was a doctor in the administration there

[14] Georgii Mikhailovich Bogachev (1880–February 1938) was born in the city of Brest-Litovsk to a family of the nobility. On August 10, 1903, he graduated from the Mikhailovskoe Artillery School, after which he was posted to the 37th Artillery Brigade. In March 1905, he was transferred to the 2nd Artillery Brigade of the Life Guards. He served in the Red Army from 1918 until 1923. He did not join the party, and lived in Leningrad. In the 1920s he was tried multiple times for "counter-revolutionary crimes," as well as facing other charges. In 1935, he was arrested again and sentenced to five years of exile as a "socially dangerous element." He served his term in the village of Zerenda in North Kazakhstan Province. In January 1938, he was arrested once more, and on February 5, 1938, was sentenced to death and shot.

[15] The Church of St Nicholas the Miracle Worker was built in Novoe Sablino in 1908, but was destroyed by fire in 1943 during the occupation. The student of the Law Faculty of the Imperial University, V. M. Bogachev, and the auditor of the Women's Medical Institute, E. V. Baskakova, were married in the church on August 26, 1912. Besides Staff-Captain Georgii Bogachev, the sponsors were Boris Borisovich Semenov, Anatolii Mikhailovich Bogachev, and Nikolai Ivanovich Negri. TsGIA SPB. F. 19. Op. 127. D. 3358. L. 50. Metricheskaia kniga tserkvi Sviatogo Nikolaia Chudotvortsa v sele Sablino.

[16] Vladimir Vladimirovich Baskakov was born on May 21, 1921. Interestingly, he was registered under his mother's surname. Central State Archive of Saint-Petersburg (TsGA SPB). F. 6143. Op. 2. D. 256. L. 169. Kniga registratsii zapisei o rozhdenii Moskovskogo raiona g. Petrograda. Later, in his military registration card issued in 1941, his surname was indicated as Baskakov-Bogachev. TsAMO RF. Kartoteka Leningradskogo voenno-peresyl'nogo punkta. Op. 530157. D. 42740. L. 311. Registratsionnaia kartochka No. 11817, August 8, 1941.

[17] A medical doctor was eligible to be conscripted for military service during the Russian Civil War. In that case, motherhood would act as a reason for exemption.

whom I knew, and who gave me a referral to an evacuation hospital in the city of Rzhev.[18] When I left Petrograd, I had deliberately traveled light, and I asked my acquaintance to give me a letter granting me permission to go home for my possessions. I spent two days at home and, again deliberately, took nothing with me.

All that I took was a few pounds of salt, which I could exchange for food at the market in Rzhev. I knew that the hospital was not yet open and that I would be able to get leave so that I could collect my goods. Once I arrived, that was how things turned out. The hospital was being set up in the huge building of the diocesan college and was still without a single bed. The personnel included three doctors and, of course, a commissar woman, who greeted me less than kindly since I had turned up late. The hospital director was Dr. Romanovskii,[19] who granted us all permission to seek lodgings in the city. For three days, I lived in the house of an officer I knew—or rather, in the house of his wife, since the officer was hiding himself somewhere. During all this time, I was wandering around, trying in every way I could think of to find a way out. In the end, I found one.

I noticed an impressive-looking building with a sign that said, "Office of the Military Commandant." I went in and approached the window. In a calm, conversational tone, I explained the situation I was in. I noted that, as the man knew, the hospital was not yet functioning. I said I needed to obtain permission and, most importantly, that I needed a letter[20] allowing me to travel to Petrograd for my possessions. . . . I handed him my identity documents, and literally within a minute, he brought me the letter. He wrote something on it, and after banging a stamp on it, handed it to me through the window . . .

I went to the hospital, and telling one of the doctors that I was going home, said I would be back in three days. I asked him not to tell anyone. Then I went to the market and bought sixty freshly laid eggs, which I placed in a little leather suitcase. My remaining things I left with the woman in my lodgings, and then set off for the railway station. On arriving home, I learned that there had been disturbances in the city and that preparations were being made for military

---

[18] This is a probably a reference to the Western Front Evacuation Point in Rzhev. An exit card records that Evdokiia Baskakova departed for her place of service on May 30, 1917. Russian State Military Archive (RGVA). Kartoteka na vybyvshikh, 7412-A. Elektronnaia kopiia: https://gwar.mil.ru/heroes/chelovek_gospital2133095/.

[19] Listed in the card-file of casualties https://gwar.mil.ru/ is the physician Mitrofan Georgievich Romanovskii.

[20] A rail pass giving the right to travel free of charge.

resistance, since General Iudenich[21] was believed to be coming. My brother-in-law, Colonel Georgii Mikhailovich Bogachev, was appointed as head of Petrograd's air defense forces. This was to save him later on, when an officer's conspiracy was revealed. He was among those arrested and was held for a long time in pre-trial detention in the Shpalernaia Prison.[22] His trial was held over three days in the premises of the former Cubat restaurant on Bol'shaia Morskaia Street, with Ul'rikh[23] presiding. Our entire family attended the trial and suffered a lot of stress. . . . I do not remember how many people were accused, but one officer was sentenced to be shot, and others to prison terms of various lengths. Our Zhorzhik was acquitted, and from the courtroom, we immediately accompanied him home to Izmailovskii Prospekt, where he and his wife Mariia Pet[rovna] had an apartment in an official building (Garnovskii's).[24] The time was three or four o'clock in the morning.

All this happened many months later, after I, having spent not three days but three weeks at home waiting for Iudenich to arrive, had gathered together

---

[21] The threat to Red Petrograd from the North-Western Army appeared in May 1919, and the high point of the fears of some and the hopes of others came in the autumn of that year. General Nikolai Nikolaevich Iudenich was in command of the North-Western Army in late June, and on October 10, began a general offensive against Petrograd. On October 15, a curfew was imposed in the city, and on October 20, a mobilization was declared. N. A. Kornatovskii, *Bor'ba za krasnyi Petrograd* (Moscow: Izd-vo AST, 2004), 329–58.

[22] The military threats of 1919, the Iudenich offensive, and the mutiny in the Krasnaia Gorka fort, as well as the Kronstadt uprising that followed in 1921, led to a feverish hunt for real and imagined conspirators. The best-known example was the affair of the "Petrograd Military Organization" in 1921. As far as is known, Georgii Bogachev was not involved in it, but he was suspected of "participation in a conspiracy in the air defense" and was arrested on August 3, 1922. By that stage, he had been fired from the army and was thus jobless; most of those who were suspected did not have any employment either. The paranoia of the young Marxist dictatorship was quite widespread: Ignatii Krachkovskii, a world-renowned Arabist, was arrested at the same time as Bogachev, for buying food from the Finns and was thus suspected of conducting espionage. The difference with the 1930s was that in the early stages of the rapidly totalitarizing Bolshevik regime, it was still possible to dispose of a false accusation, which is exactly what happened to Bogachev and Krachkovskii. After spending a few months in jail, both were eventually released. TsGA SPB. F. 1930. Op. 1. D. 5. L. 12. Kartoteka lits, lishennykh izbiratel'nykh prav; TsGA SPB. F. 8912. Op. 1. D. 5. L. 12, 53. Spiski sledstvennykh del, hakhodiashchikhsia v 1 Spetsotdele KRO; A. A. Dolinina, *Nevol'nik dolga: Nauchnaia biografiia akademika I. Iu. Krachkovskogo* (Saint-Petersburg: Tsents "Peterburgskoe Vostokovedenie," 1994), 120–23. Since 1875 until the present day, a well-known remand prison has been located on Ulitsa Shpalernaia. In the early years of the twentieth century, it was known as the House of Pretrial Detention.

[23] Vasilii Vasil'evich Ul'rikh (1889–1951) was a prominent Soviet functionary, military leader, and colonel-general of justice. The military prosecutor of Petrograd mentioned in his report that the case of the "counterrevolutionary officer conspiracy" was investigated by the Field Team of the Higher Court, headed by Ul'rikh. In 1920, the building housing Pierre Cubat's famous restaurant (Café de Paris) was turned into the Red Army Club, one of the potential places for holding a public trial. TsGA SPB. F. 8912b. Op. 1. D. 7. L. 23. Doklad voennogo prokurora Petrogradskogo voennogo okruga Sliosberga, March 25, 1923.

[24] The barracks of the Life Guards of the Izmailovskii Regiment on the corner of Izmailovskii Prospekt and the Fontanka Embankment.

various items that I could exchange for foodstuffs in Rzhev, and had set off back to the place where I was serving. There, of course, "thunders and lightnings" awaited me. I had been put on trial in my absence before a military tribunal, and my punishment was as follows: I was to organize an infirmary for soldiers infected with typhus, to care for them, and to live next to them, without leaving the territory of the hospital. While I was away, more doctors had arrived, and one of them had been appointed head physician. This was a doctor named Shpolianskii, who was also displeased *with me*,[25] since it had earlier been assumed that I would fill this role. Later, he and I became good friends and lived in the same apartment on the bank of the Volga. Soon the entire hospital was turned over to treating typhus, and in my infirmary, I was accommodating only medical personnel. Over the space of a year, many people stayed there, but thanks to the care they received, relatively few of them died. I remember how perhaps once a week I would have to deliver a eulogy in the cemetery.

The city of Rzhev had a population of Old Believers, and in an apartment where I lived for two months, I got to observe their life. I found them a strange and disagreeable kind of people. As time passed, several doctors went on leave, but I was told that I was not even to dream of going on leave myself. At the end of the year, just before Christmas, Dr. Shpolianskii fell ill as well, and was admitted to my infirmary. He was sick for quite a long time, but thanks to the care he was given, did not suffer from complications.

We held a Christmas Eve celebration next to his bed. There was a marvelous fir tree standing on a table. One of the doctors brought three wax candles that he had stolen from a church. Everything was very cozy and jolly. We sang, recited, and told various stories. The whole company sat and relaxed, scratching themselves and occasionally, when they had caught a louse, dropping it behind the glass of the kerosene lamp.

Soon Dr. Shpolianskii informed me that there was not a thermometer to be had anywhere in the city, and that this question had his superiors very worried. I had long been telling Shpolianskii that my husband had a hundred of them. The thought immediately dawned on me that I could go on a trip to fetch them, and I promptly wrote to my husband, asking if he still had them. He sent a telegram saying that he had fallen ill with typhus and was waiting for me. Dr. Shpolianskii put in a request for Dr. Baskakova to be released so that she could go and obtain the thermometers. When the Rzhev city execu-

---

[25] Words in italics are crossed out in the original text.

tive committee heard my name, they refused to grant me permission to make the trip. But the need was so great that they eventually gave me ten days' leave, with Dr. Shpolianskii having to vouch for my return. He did so, after obtaining from me my word of honor.

While living in Rzhev, I had continuously accumulated food provisions, and by the time of my departure I already had a whole plywood box, 20 pounds in weight, full of meat alone. In a shoulder bag I had groats, flour, jugs of clarified butter, and a tin of sunflower oil. Assigned to accompany me was an orderly from near Luga. He carried the rucksack while I looked after my plywood box. We traveled by way of Moscow, since I wanted to visit my Baskakova-Bogacheva sister, the wife of my husband's older brother. My brother-in-law, I knew, was being held in prison as a person of wealth.[26] He was later released, though Trotskii[27] confiscated his wonderful Orel racehorse, named "Volchek," that had won prizes at the racecourse. This brother-in-law, Nikolai, hanged himself many years later, never having found a place for himself in life.[28]

At the railway station in Moscow, a Latvian woman[29] came close to seizing all the meat, but I showed her the telegram indicating that my husband was ill in Petrograd, where the food situation was regarded as worse than in Moscow. At home, everything was in order. We lived at that time where I had worked, at the hospital of the Aleksandrovskaia Community of the Red Cross at 9 Ulitsa Bronnitskaia. Later, this hospital came to bear the name of Engels.[30] The sisters and all the workers said my arrival was very fortunate, since on that same day a huge quantity of firewood had been delivered to meet the needs of the hospital, and had been heaped up on the corner of our street and Zagorodnyi Prospekt. Everyone joined in the work of shifting it. I helped in this, even though I was dressed in a beautiful coat that my

---

[26] The reference is to the early repression carried out against the wealthy and privileged classes.

[27] Lev Davidovich Trotskii (1879–1940) was one of the leading Bolsheviks. A revolutionary and military strategist, he became an emigrant and was the founder of Trotskyism.

[28] Nikolai Mikhailovich Bogachev is shown in the 1914 Moscow address book as living at 13 Kuznetskii Most. *Vsia Moskva*, 916.

[29] The Latvian riflemen were among the symbols of the Civil War in Russia. Described in this case was a woman who was most likely a member of a Red Guard patrol looking for "speculators." Baskakova may actually have recognized the woman as Latvian, but it is also possible that the ethnic marker was used to designate her social role.

[30] The Engels Hospital was established in 1918 on the basis of the Aleksandrovskaia Community of the Sisters of Mercy of the Russian Society of the Red Cross, in connection with its transfer from the Red Cross to the State Healthcare Organization. In 1920, it came to be known as Infirmary No. 11, until in December of that year when the name of Friedrich Engels was bestowed upon it. In 1925, it was again transferred to the Red Cross, under whose administration it remained until 1932.

husband had bought for me in the Mertens store,[31] when its stock was sold off and the store was closed.

Time passed, however, and it was necessary to depart. Quietly, on foot, we proceeded to the military commandant's office on Italianskaia Ulitsa. There I showed my documents, but the official demanded proof that I had fulfilled the aim of my trip. I set off homeward, happy that, through no fault of my own, I would be delayed for another day. There at home, guests who had been invited to share a meal of steak with us were waiting. They included Gospodin[32] Zamkov, a friend of Dr. Shpolianskii. I sat and watched sadly as they all dived in. All I wanted was for them to go. I sat in a deep English armchair, dressed in my new coat, even though everyone said that it was warm [in the house].

During the evening, my husband brought one of the thermometers and jokingly forced me to try it. My temperature was 40 degrees. I jumped up delightedly, exclaiming: "Thank God, I've got typhus, and I'm at home!" My orderly arrived, and I entrusted the thermometers to him, asking him to hand them on to Dr. Shpolianskii. The latter, of course, believed me, but the administrators, naturally, did not. After a short while, a doctor from the military commandant's office visited me, but I was delirious and did not remember him. He went away convinced that I had typhus, which indeed I was not feigning.

After I had recovered, I did not present myself for re-examination for another six months, although I was piled with summonses from the Petrograd Department of the Military-Sanitary Administration. During that time, I was elected from the Obukhovskaia Hospital, and from ours as well, as a member of the Petrograd Soviet of Workers and Red Army Deputies. Lying before me now is the red booklet, Certificate No. 677: "The bearer, Baskakova Evdokiia Vasil'evna, is a member of the Petrograd Soviet of the Sixth Convocation (second half of 1920). Chairman—Zinov'ev."[33]

Nevertheless, I was obliged during the autumn to go to Minsk, where to my delight the secretary was the same doctor whom I knew from Smolensk. I spent the night in his apartment, and in the morning, we set off. I felt dreadful, since I had a toothache, and my cheek was swollen. My acquaintance promised that in recommending me to the chief, whose name was Lenskii, he would make

---

[31] The trading house of the Mertens fur products firm, on Nevskii Prospekt, was built in 1911. In 1944, it became the first *Dom modelei* in the USSR.

[32] Polite Russian form of "sir."

[33] Grigorii Evseevich Zinov'ev (1883–1936) was one of the top leaders of the VKP(b) and head of the Petrograd Soviet at this time.

sure that he [the chief] would prefer to engage someone else from other doctors who had arrived at the same time. Later, he told me what he had reported. Everything had been brought to bear: how busy I was with my activity in the Petrograd Soviet; my "graviditas,"[34] which I was finding difficult; and other minuses. When I came face to face with Lenskii, who knew about my trial in Rzhev, I assumed an even more miserable expression, and . . . was granted permission to travel home and to register with the Petrograd Department of the Military-Sanitary Administration. For a long time after I registered with the administration, I was subjected to attempts to send me off to serve in one place or another, until the legal duration of my pregnancy was up, and I was set free entirely.

During this time, the Society of the Red Cross began to collapse, which of course immediately affected the Communities of the Sisters of Mercy with their hospitals and their vast property holdings. Our community was the Aleksandrovskaia, whose holy patron was St. Aleksandr Nevskii, and whose *unholy* patron was Evgenii Vasil'evich Pavlov,[35] who had been appointed as *leib-khirurg* [surgeon-general] after the Beilis trial.[36] I had gotten to know him and worked under his direction from late in 1914 until early in 1916, when in appalling pain (the orderly on duty was constantly taking a loaded revolver from him), he died from gas cellulitis in his left arm. Tragically, in that pre-antibiotic age, there was no miracle-working penicillin, and treatment was limited either to complete amputation of a limb or to massive excision of the whole thickness of the swollen tissue. At his consultation, Evgenii Vasil'evich was completely clearheaded and agreed to the excision being made, but on the condition that Professor Tseidler[37] should perform the operation, while the anesthetic should be administered by Dr. Baskakova E[vdokia] V[asil'evna].

---

[34]   Pregnancy (*Latin*).

[35]   Evgenii Vasil'evich Pavlov (1845–1916) was a doctor of medicine, professor of the Military Medical Academy, and head of St. Alexander's Women's Hospital after 1895.

[36]   The Beilis affair was an anti-Semitic trial that took place in 1911, when Menakhem Beilis was accused of the ritual murder of the gymnasium student Andrei Iushchinskii. Evgenii Vasil'evich Pavlov acted as an expert witness for the defense during the trial. Also involved here is a dubious pun, based on the similar sound of the German word *Leib* and the Jewish name Leib, or Leiba in its Russian pronunciation. It should be noted that in pre-revolutionary society, anti-Semitism, as a background element of consciousness on which few Russians ever reflected, was close to the norm.

[37]   German Ferdinandovich Tseidler (1861–1929/1940?) was a surgeon, professor at the Medical Institute for Women, and both head of faculty and director of the Institute's surgical clinic. After the revolution, he emigrated to Finland. M. Kostolomov, *Tsvety na koliuchei vetke: Krasnyi krest zhiznennogo puti professora Tsaidlera; Wiborgiana Kraevedcheskie ocherki* (Kerama: Kerammiks, 2010).

He chose me because he valued my knowledge and experience, after having observed my work in administering chloroform or ether on an almost daily basis. He then asked me to keep an eye on Tseidler, and not to let him get carried away [with the process of cutting out flesh], adding on his own account, "since I'm still going to work." We can only be thankful that Pavlov did not have to endure the total destruction of his "child," the Red Cross organization itself.

I recall that I was elected as a delegate to the congress in Moscow, and that before this, noisy meetings of the "workers of the Red Cross" were held in the Sheremet'ev Palace on the Fontanka Embankment. My task was to somehow reconcile the ultra-red workers of the "Red Cross stores" with the staff of the "administration," that is, the officials and medical personnel. Everyone now knows what came of this.[38] The hospital held out for another two years, because my husband came up with the idea of founding a union, but one made up solely of doctors and of sisters of mercy with extensive experience, that is, the senior nursing sisters, the ones with the cross.[39] There remained many younger sisters who were anxious to complete the course, since they had lived in the [Old Believer] community. The revolution had freed them from their secluded life, and they could now go out freely, visit theatres, go to dances, and attend meetings.[40]

My husband sought to provide the hospital with paying patients and concluded a contract with the water transport health care organization. We witnessed the destruction and plunder of our marvelous church, with its white marble iconostasis. With two liters of surgical spirit from the pharmacy, my husband managed to preserve the shine of the Italian crystal. When I was expecting my child, the pious old sisters asked me to confess and take communion. During the confession, I replied to almost all the questions, "No, I have not sinned," and our old priest kept telling me, "Hubris, you are too full of hubris."

---

[38] The All-Russian Union of the Sisters of Mercy, which united all the communities of the Red Cross, was merged in May 1919 with the trade unions of medical workers, after which the sisters of mercy were transformed *de facto* into nurses, that is, service personnel. A. V. Sribnaia, "Organizatsiia deiatel'nosti sester miloserdiia v gody Pervoi mirovoi voiny," *Vestnik PSTGU, Seriia II*, no. 5 (60) (2014): 70–87.

[39] The senior nursing sisters, the ones "with the cross," were those who had worked for five or six years and who had undergone an additional course of training. They wore a cross on a chain about their necks.

[40] Under the pre-revolutionary statutes of the Russian Society of the Red Cross, sisters of mercy did not have the right to marry and lived in relatively spartan circumstances. The young sisters were generally uneducated.

In Pushkin: Memory Snapshots

Excerpts have been published from the diary of Osipova,[41] the so-called "internal émigré" who lived in the city of Pushkin during its occupation by the Germans. These excerpts aroused a swarm of recollections in me, most of them painful.[42]

In her writings, Gospozha Osipova mentions the writer Beliaev,[43] and I felt a strong urge to go back in my memory and recall several meetings I had with this wonderfully interesting man. I saw him and talked with him for the last time a few days before his tragic death.[44] Gospozha Osipova notes *quite correctly*[45] in her text that when you are starving, it is a great mistake to lie down.... Beliaev, who was starving, lay down, did not have the strength to fetch firewood, which everyone at that time had in abundance, and . . . froze to death. Beliaev's death was a double and even triple tragedy.

First, he died at a time when his talent as a writer was flourishing, and at a time when he could have had the possibility of writing whatever he wanted. He told me how the Soviet authorities had forced him to change the epilogue of his book *The Man Who Found His Face* or else they would refuse to let it appear in print, as a flagrantly cosmopolitan work. He was waiting from day to day for the German commandant of the city of Pushkin to fulfill a promise to send him to Pskov to edit a Russian-language newspaper.[46]

---

[41] Olimpiada Georgievna Poliakova (1902–1958), who wrote under the pseudonym "Lidiia Osipova," was a commentator, literary scholar, second-wave émigré, and activist of the National Labor Alliance of Russian Solidarists (NTS). She was born in Novocherkassk, and in 1919 married Nikolai Poliakov. Prior to the Second World War, she and her husband settled in Pushkin. She worked for the collaborationist press, and in 1944 was evacuated to Germany. Along with her husband, she joined the Popular Labor Union. Following the end of the war she remained in the American zone of occupation, and around 1950, using the pseudonym Lidiia Osipova, prepared for the press her "Diary of a Collaborator," recording details of life under the occupation. Excerpts were published four years later. She died in Oberammergau in 1958.

[42] This perhaps refers to the publication in 1954 of some of Poliakova's reminiscences in the journal *Grani*.

[43] Aleksandr Romanovich Beliaev (1884–1942) was a journalist, Soviet writer, and one of the founders of the genre of science fiction in Russia. He was born in Smolensk, graduated from law school, and for many years worked as a lawyer. Involving himself in literature and the theatre, he turned to serious literary work in the 1920s, and from 1928 was a professional writer. From 1932 he lived in Pushkin with his third wife Margarita Magnushevskaia, daughter Svetlana, and mother-in-law El'vira Magnushevskaia. He was the author of 18 novels.

[44] As recalled by his wife, Beliaev died on January 6, 1942. The same date is indicated in the notebook of Razumnik Ivanov-Razumnik: Tsypin, *Gorod Pushkin v gody voiny*, 195; Amherst College, MA. Amherst Center for Russian Culture. The Archive Collection. The R. V. Ivanov-Razumnik Diary of 1942 (hereafter Amherst College/The Ivanov-Razumnik diary). Zapisnaia knizhka na 1942 god. 1/I. Tsarskoe Selo (Pushkin). Entry from January 6, 1942, page 10.

[45] Words in italics are crossed out in the original text.

[46] This information here is found nowhere else. Traditionally, Beliaev's death has been cited as an example of the inhumanity of the occupation regime. Evidence of his agreement to collaborate with the Germans has never been published before.

Incidentally, this request of mine concerning Beliaev was forwarded to the commandant by the exact same interpreter of whom Osipova speaks so unflatteringly, but for some reason she calls this woman Klara Ivanovna, while in fact she was Ol'ga Ivanovna Videman.[47] Klara was her sister, a quiet, inoffensive woman who had a Russian surname, having married a former Russian priest, and who was later on to suffer grievously at the hands of her cruel, domineering younger sibling.[48]

---

[47] Ol'ga Ivanovna Videman and her two daughters occupy a conspicuous place in Baskakova's text. Ol'ga's maiden name was Kaspersen; she was born in 1884 to the family of a stationmaster of the Warsaw railway, and studied at the Mariinskaia gymnasium. In 1923, she married Vol'demar Edmundovich Videman, the son of a Tallinn merchant of German extraction; that same year, Vol'demar had graduated from the Technological Institute in Leningrad. Within a year a daughter, Jenni (Zhenia) was born to them. It is possible that before the war Ol'ga worked for the Institute of the Milk Industry; in June 1941, the Pushkin city newspaper, in a note on the organizing of a sanitary brigade, mentioned a female staff member named Videman. Ol'ga's husband, Vol'demar, was most likely repressed; the International Memorial database lists an engineer of that name who was arrested on September 9, 1941, and who died in prison in Chistopol' in 1943. In the lists of the Soviet commission charged with determining losses, Ol'ga Videman is stated to have died as a result of shelling. She was alive in April 1943, when she placed an advertisement in the Tallinn newspaper *Severnoe Slovo* trying to locate another resident of Pushkin, Yanina Baranovich. She was subsequently evacuated to Riga and in late 1944 she and her daughters were residing in Kassel at their Germans relative's, Generalstabartzt Alexander von Remus (1887–1964). According to a letter from her sister, Videman was a camp commandant (*Lagerführerin*). A. Feoktistov, "Zhenshchiny-patriotki," *Bol'shevistskoe Slovo*, no. 72, June 26, 1941; TsGA SPB. F. 3355. Op. 10. D. 44. L. 17. Akty-spiski zhitelei g. Pushkin, 1944; TsGA SPB. F. 6143. Op. 3. D. 300. L. 136. Kniga registratsii zapisei aktov grazhdanskogo sostoianiia v Moskovsko-Narvskom raione Petrograda, 22.02.1923; TsGA SPB. F. 6143. Op. 4. D. 59. L. 50. Kniga registratsii zapisei o rozhdenii Moskovsko-Narvskogo raiona, zapis' No. 550, 28.10.1924; Ob'iavlenie O. I. Videman. *Severnoe Slovo*, no. 44 (136), April 16, 1943; TsGIA SPB. F. 346. Op. 1. D. 119. L. 48. Attestat Kaspersen Ol'gi Ivanovny, 1905; TsGIA SPB. F. 492. Op. 2. D. 8082. L. 1, 22. O priniatii v studenty 1-go. kursa Vol'demara Videmana, 1904–1923; Bundesarchiv Berlin (hereafter BArch Berlin), R/9361-IV, 5702, Bl. 13. Klara Axenoff an Bannmädelührerin Hoffman, September 3, 1944.

[48] The witness Anna Zorina, interrogated by the NKVD after the liberation of Pushkin, made the same error: "Working as an interpreter at that time was Klara Ivanovna, who earlier had been a German language teacher in a school." Klara Ivanovna was born on May 15, 1881, graduated from the Ekaterininskaia gymnasium, and in 1905 began working at the Aleksandrovskaia Women's Gymnasium, first as a form mistress, and then as a teacher of German. Between 1914 and 1916, she taught at the prestigious Tenishevskoe College, where the students at that time included the future Nobel nominee Vladimir Nabokov. After that she appears to have taught at home. Klara married Petr Stepanovich Aksenov, who merits attention in his own right. Petr Aksenov, who was born on June 23, 1872, actually served as a priest from 1904 to 1911. He joined the "circle of the 32," a group of St. Petersburg clerics who called for reforms to the church administration, and who are regarded as precursors of the renewal movement that founded its own church in the 1920s. He was a member of the Religious-Philosophical Society, a writer, and a journalist. After leaving the church in 1911, he graduated from the Law Faculty of St. Petersburg University and worked as a lawyer and schoolteacher. Following the revolution, he concentrated on his pedagogical career, teaching literature in various schools and, in 1924, in the Leningrad Home for Juvenile Delinquents. In 1929, he had settled with his wife in Pushkin (Detskoe Selo). He evidently managed to conceal his past in the clergy and "reactionary circles," since he had not been a priest since 1917 and had published his writings under pseudonyms. A 1930 employment list notes only his work as a teacher. In 1931, their only child, a teenage girl of fifteen years, perished from meningitis. In February 1942, the Aksenovs left for Germany, being included in a list of *Volksdeutsche*, along with Ol'ga Videman and her daughters. They were billeted in a camp in Konice together with Ivanov-

Beliaev's second tragedy was that at the same time as he was starving, he was bedridden as a result of his chronic illness, tuberculous spondylitis. Even earlier, in peacetime, this had meant that he could barely walk and was unable to look after his needs. It was on account of his illness that I became acquainted with him two years before the war. I was not a tuberculosis surgeon, and he was being examined by other specialists, but once he was also diagnosed with a different surgical condition, a hernia, and I then tended to him as a consultant surgeon of the Pushkin polyclinic.

His third tragedy was that in the first days of the occupation, his wife, a strong, healthy woman, found work in one of the German kitchens. She herself was, of course, well fed, and she brought home soup, crusts of bread, and frozen potatoes that the Germans themselves would not eat. But here the wife and mother came up against a dilemma: whom should she feed? Or rather, to whom should she give the best and largest portions—to her husband, or to her daughter? She gave them to her daughter. In peacetime, I had witnessed her constant care for her sick husband, to whom she was at the same time nurse, sister of mercy, and typist of his works. She showed a great concern for her 11-year-old daughter Svetlana, who at that time had already begun to show signs of a hereditary disease that in the prewar period had spread to involve tuberculosis of the cavity of the knee joint. Because of this, and attending to her in her home, I had put a plaster cast on her whole leg. I recall the horror and displea-

---

Razumnik. In December 1942, the Aksenovs were sent to a camp near Chełm, in the vicinity of Lublin, and in April 1943, they made it back to occupied Soviet territory, to Ostrov, which is south of Pskov. The latter unexpected return happened thanks to Vladimir Aksenov, the son from Petr's first marriage and a lawyer by training, who was an active collaborator and attained the position of the district mayor (*Rayonchef*) in Ostrov. Klara thus worked as an interpreter. With the German armies retreating from the USSR, the Aksenovs and their son were evacuated to Riga, whence in the summer of 1944 Klara, a gravely sick Petr, and their granddaughter Nina left for Danzig. In Germany, Klara made attempts to secure a job as a schoolteacher and lived in poverty. The latter fates of the Aksenovs remain unclear. TsGA SPB F. 8557. Op. 6. D. 1095. L. 45. Protokol doprosa Zorinoi Anny Ivanovny, February 29, 1944; TsGIA SPB. F. 15. Op. 2. D. 480. L. 1–30. Lichnoe delo Kaspersen Klary Ivanovny, 1906; TsGIA SPB. F. 176. Op. 2. D. 102. L. 2–3, 11. Khodataistvo Klary Ivanovny Kaspersen (Kaspersen) na imia direktora Tenishevskogo uchilishcha, August 1914, 26, Udostoverenie ot 3 iiulia 1920; I. F. Masanov, *Slovar' psevdonimov russkikh pisatelei, uchenykh i obshchestvennykh deiatelei*, vol. 4 (Moscow, 1960), 30; Iuliia Balakshina, *Bratsvo revnitelei tserkovnogo obnovleniia (gruppa "332-kh" peterburgskikh sviashchennikov), 1903–1907* (Moscow: Sviato-Filaretovskii Institut, 2015), 59–63; Iu. L. Orekhanov, "K rannei istorii obnovlenchestva: Spisok chlenov 'Bratstva revnitelei tserkovnogo obnovleniia,' sostoiashchikh v sviashchennom sane," in *Bogoslovskii sbornik Pravoslavnogo Sviato-Tikhonovskogo bogoslovskogo instituta*, no. 3b (Moscow, 1999), 222; TsGA SPB. F. 7409. Op. 28. D. 25. L. 26–31. Aksov-Aksenov Petr Ionovich, trudovoi spisok, 1930; TsGA SPB. F. 3355. Op. 10. D. 44. L. 13. Spiski naseleniia (Pushkin), bez daty; BArch Berlin, R/9361-IV, 4072. Klara Axionoff, Lebenslauf, July 25, 1942; BArch Berlin, R/9361-IV, 5702, Bl. 5. Bannmädelführerin Hoffman an der Reichskommissar für die Festigung deutschen Volkstums, July 22, 1944; Bundesarchiv—Militärarchiv Freiburg (hereafter BArch Freiburg), 20–18/1005, Bl. 114. AOK 18, Abt. Ic, Schreiben des russischen Rechtsanwalts Wladimir Aksenow, Ssablino, January 16, 1942.

sure of the girl's parents, and her own immediate joy, when she received a pair of crutches and was then able even to leap up the stairs on them. At that time, they lived on the second or third floor, and occupied a three-room apartment with a kitchen and bathroom. There were only four of them: Aleksandr Romanovich, his wife, their daughter, and his wife's mother.[49]

As a doctor in the Pushkin polyclinic, I was obliged almost every day to observe the domestic life of the 55-thousand-strong population of this "city of the muses," where for the "muses" not even a single corner was left in the parks. There, the elegant pavilions and other structures were all occupied by "martyr-residents." In winter, these people suffered from the cold, from lack of water, and from remoteness from means of transport, while in summer they were beset by swarms of mosquitoes and by crowds of tourists on excursions.[50]

I recall how happy I was when I got the chance to visit that district. As a consulting surgeon, I had access to a car, and this delivered me smoothly and quietly to the spot along the beautiful broad roads of the park, or forced me to endure tragicomic moments as I got my feet soaked while sitting in this same vehicle. The road around the circumference of the parks was appalling, and when it rained there were places (next to the Great Caprice[51]) where lakes of water formed along with liquid mud. Even when I was traveling cautiously with an experienced driver (Comrade Uskov), the water rose above the footboard and poured into the cabin. The Beliaevs' apartment was in the center of the city, near the Avangard cinema (earlier, the cinema had borne a name from Russian antiquity, "Teremok," and this name had accordingly been dispensed with. The Soviets changed the name but not the décor, and throughout all those years the place had not been renovated even once.).[52]

When I visited the Beliaevs, I did not make use of the car, since if I had, I would have needed to keep the visit extremely brief in order not to keep the vehicle waiting, and my visits to Aleksandr Romanovich never took up less than an hour.

---

[49] Baskakova implies that theirs was a "luxurious" Soviet life. Standard living space in the city was 4.5 square meters per person and usually in a communal apartment, with multiple families living in it (one family per room). Basic human necessities, such as the indoor plumbing, were signs of prosperity and a reason for envy.

[50] Living in the premises of the palace-museums were numerous workers with their families, and also random people. The fact that the building of the Tsarskoe Selo college was both a tourism site and a dwelling-place was inevitably disturbing to the residents and was the subject of repeated remarks and comment pieces in the city newspaper.

[51] An artificial hill with a tunnel that connected the Aleksandrovskii and Ekaterininskii parks.

[52] The building has been preserved; the Avangard cinema is located at Ulitsa Moskovskaia, dom 32/17. In 1925, Evdokiia Baskakova's husband worked as the manager of the private (leased) Anons cinema in Leningrad. TsGA SPB. F. 1963. Op. 1. D. 95b. L. 167. Patent Bogacheva V. M. ot 2 marta 1925.

During this time, he and I had to work out the state of his health, while he made so many observations about himself as an invalid, and volunteered so many bits of knowledge about medicine and the biological sciences in general that, I must confess, I sometimes found it difficult dealing with this "know-it-all," though at the same time it was very interesting and instructive. After exhausting these medical topics, we passed on to literature. I might say that before I became personally acquainted with this author, I had read almost none of his writings. I had a grown son who should have been familiar with him, but even this was not the case.

Our family as a whole were great lovers of books, especially my husband, who was an out-and-out bibliophile. We built up a library of more than three thousand volumes that were burnt together with the building and all our other possessions on the fifth day after the Germans arrived, while we huddled in the basement of the 1st School, hiding now from the Russian bombs and shell-fire. Earlier, when the shells that were bursting were of German origin, we were holed up in the building of the Pushkin polyclinic and in its bomb shelter, since this was where I worked as chief surgeon and head of the traumatological department. At the last minute, the fleeing party leadership awarded me the title of chief medical officer. This was only for a few days, of course, while they held off the German front ...

On September 9, I traveled to Leningrad for the last time to attend to my second job with the medical department of the water transport authority.[53] The rail journey now required a special pass. My work colleagues met me with horror and ... secret envy, while frightening me by talking of what might happen if I did not manage to return home.

Nevertheless, I made the return trip successfully enough. Blowing in through the open windows of the carriage on the way was the sickly-sweet smell of smoke from the continuing fire in the Badaevskii warehouses.[54] The passengers were grumbling, sadly and indignantly, that for years we had received nothing and that now jam and sugar were going up in flames. Stretching along both sides of the railway line were groups of people with carts, with bundles, and with children, and it was unclear where they were fleeing. Into the city? Out of the city?

---

[53] The reference is to her role as a doctor in the provincial polyclinic of the water transport workers at Universitetskaia Naberezhnaia, dom 25.

[54] Following a bombardment on September 8, 1941, the Badaevskii warehouses burned down. The reserves of food that were destroyed were not so great as to decisively affect the fate of the city's residents, but the fire became a symbol of the beginning of the blockade, and served in popular memory as a fateful pointer to the catastrophic hunger that was to follow.

On September 10 and 11, they shelled our Pushkin too. The result of the bombardment was a large number of people suffering from wounds and burns, and the order was given for all surgeons to gather in the city hospital to provide aid. In the hospital, the main operating theater and the premises adjacent to it had been destroyed by a shell the previous day (some smart people had decided to place a gun on the roof and set up an observation post).

Everywhere, among the fragments of plaster, were stretchers and beds with moaning patients. The most intense work was being performed in the dressing station, where surgeons and their assistants were operating on ten tables. I set to work as well, and from where I was, had a spat with the chief registrar, Dr. Kartblium.

As usual, she had set about instructing and demonstrating. The head surgeon, Professor S., took my side and asked her to postpone her lectures until a better moment, and for the present, to do her job and let others work as well, since he and other staff members needed to catch a train at 5 o'clock in the morning, evidently the last train. I don't know whether the professor reached Leningrad on the train or on foot, or whether the poor man made it at all.[55]

Dr. Kartblium, along with me and many other medical staff, remained in Pushkin. We doctors organized a hospital in the House of Veterans of the Revolution (the Kochubei Palace), where she was the chief medical officer, since in the first place she was a good specialist in her field, and second, had an excellent grasp of the German language, since she was German herself. The poor woman allowed herself to be lured by an enticing offer of the Germans into going to Germany to deepen her knowledge of blood transfusions, a topic she had long studied. She left for Pskov by car, and I said a heartfelt goodbye to her. I spent the whole night talking with her, since I was lying in her room after an operation under full anesthesia following a blood transfusion that Dr. Gracheva[56] administered to me. I was suffering from cellulitis in my hand following a cut to a finger, and of course as a result of hunger I was at risk of a blood infection, which indeed had set in. Two years later, when I was already in Germany, I learned that Dr. Kartblium was in a psychiatric hospital in the

---

[55] In 1941, Associate Professor Osher Abramovich Sternin (1890–after 1945) was head of the surgical section of the city hospital. As a Jew, he had every reason to hurry in order not to end up under the Germans, but he managed to make it to Leningrad. Later, he headed an evacuation hospital, and finished the war with the rank of major in the medical service.

[56] The identity of this person could not be established. It is known that on August 9, 1943, a Russian doctor with the surname Gracheva was transferred from Gatchina to the Siverskii Hospital. TsGA SPB. F.3355. Op. 4. D. 236. L. 2. Kommandant des rückwärtigen Armeegebiets 583 O.U. den 9.08.43.

city of Königsberg. It was said that she had been forced to work on the question of blood transfusions in concentration camps, and as a result . . . had finished up in a mental hospital.[57]

During those same days, I called on the Beliaevs and told them that it would be safer for them to move to the bottom floor. There were many empty apartments since people were fleeing in every direction. I remember that Aleksandr Romanovich went out onto the little balcony and pointed to a tree, a very tall one, saying that if the place were bombed and the exits were destroyed, he would climb over onto the tree and lower himself down. Fate, however, did not allow him to do this. A bomb was indeed to destroy the entire wing of three floors where his apartment was located.

I also visited them after the arrival of the Germans, precisely in connection with his work on a Russian-language newspaper (so that the Germans would understand the genre in which he wrote, I persuaded the interpreter to recommend Beliaev as a "Russian Jules Verne"), and this time found them in a different apartment. It turned out that they had moved to the bottom floor of the wing, with an exit that led not onto the courtyard, as before, but onto the street. Many things, and most importantly books, had to be left in the old apartment, since the family lacked the strength to take much with them. Aleksandr Romanovich told me that he had selected a basketful of books for me, his own works and some medical texts, and that they had been left beneath the staircase. I never took them, and then the staircase and the building were destroyed. He drank a glass of milk that I had brought for him only when I told him that I would drink the milk if he did not. Tellingly, he glanced at the door that led into the kitchen, where Svetlana and her grandmother were at that moment.

They are here: Start of the German occupation

Soon after the Germans arrived in Pushkin, that is, on September 17, 1941 (not on September 19, as Lidiia Osipova writes), they for some reason seized all available fodder and hay from the population and from the city storehouses. This was followed by the confiscation of cows. Many owners surrendered their livestock out of fear of the conquerors, and because there was nothing with

---

[57] In 1938, Ingeborg Ivanovna Karlblom (whose name Baskakova misspells as Kartblium) headed the city blood transfusion center, and in 1940 and 1941 was a doctor in the city hospital. She was regarded as a valued worker; in 1939 a laudatory article in the city newspaper was devoted to her. N. Markov, "Sovetskii vrach," *Bol'shevistskoe Slovo*, no. 45, April 9, 1939, 3.

which to feed the animals in any case (since early October frosts had been occurring, without any snow, and the pastures had also vanished). Other owners directed indignant complaints to the commandant, while yet others made
haste to secretly slaughter their cows and to salt or smoke the meat. Some of
these people got away with it, but the commandant ordered one of my patients
to be whipped in a stable, and for a long time Sister Bednova[58] went to her to
bandage her wounds. Incidentally, the woman concerned was acquainted with
the commandant's assistant, and pleaded for the execution of the sentence not
to be too harsh. The assistant, however, bellowed with laughter and suggested
that she simply wrap up her corresponding spot [buttocks] in something soft.[59]

A few of the owners, however, acted more advisedly, and appealed directly
to the "all-powerful Olga Ivanovna" [Videman], hinting to her that she would
never have to drink coffee without milk. I do not know on whose initiative it
was decided to create a shared space for 30 remaining cows that were allotted
a ration of hay, but which the owners themselves cared for and milked. In addition to the owner, others were involved (Dr. Korovin, *a veterinarian*[60]), actually Dr. Urtaev.[61]

The idyll of the cows did not last long; the commandant, along with Ol'ga Ivanovna and her extensive retinue of German visitors, never had his coffee without milk. In the German units, the half-starved soldiers weren't asleep either,
and on three occasions carried out raids on the dairy and took away a number
of cows. Before the commandant took the wise decision to eat the rest himself,
I enlisted the same Ol'ga Ivanovna in arranging permission for one of my acquaintances to remove her cow on the grounds that it was "sick," so that a veterinarian could make use of it at home. I should state that back in the time of
NEP this woman was a janitor at the house at 7 Moskovskaia Ulitsa, which my
husband leased for five years and which was completely renovated after being
occupied barbarously by one of the numerous children's homes (at the beginning of Bolshevik rule, Tsarskoe Selo had been renamed "Detskoe Selo" [Chil-

---

[58] The identity of this person could not be established. A hairdresser named Dmitrii Bednov, born in 1900, was living in Pushkin. TsGA SPB. F. 3355. Op. 10. D. 265. L. 65; Istorii bolezni patsientov Pavlovskoi bol'nitsy, 09.09.1941.

[59] Olimpiada Poliakova in her diary also expressed outrage at the whipping of young women in police custody. Budnitskii and Zelenina, *"Svershilos'. Prishli nemtsy!,"* 149.

[60] Words in italics are crossed out in the original text.

[61] The ending of this sentence is written by hand. In her writings, Poliakova uses pseudonyms, and refers to Urtaev as "Korovin." Baskakova reveals who the people were, though she herself desig-nates some people by their initials.

dren's Village]).[62] In this house that dated from the time of Catherine the Great we lived peacefully for five years, and when the term of the lease and NEP itself came to an end, we first tried to reduce our living space, renting out one of the halves to the writer Shishkov[63] at the insistent request of the writer Aleksei Tolstoi.[64] But the city soviet continued reducing our living space, and we decided to move to 11 Moskovskoe Shosse.

From these distant times my former janitor Fekla Grigor'evna Rogach had retained a strong attachment to all my family, and in gratitude for the fact that in times past we had helped her to live in a fashion worthy of a human being and to raise her three daughters, she saw it as her direct obligation to help us in our famished misery. Even before the arrival of the Germans, when difficulties had already appeared with food supplies, she supplied my family with milk, and of course, continued doing this later on.

When she was permitted to take her source of food and drink and return it to its old stall, the next round of fears began, since suspicious soldiers circled round about, asking about the milk, but she somehow refused them. Incidentally, I have the impression that it was precisely my Fekla Grigor'evna who features in the writings of Lidiia Osipova as the woman who refused outright to sell milk to the sick artist Klever.[65]

---

[62] Vladimir Bogachev wrote about the repairs and the considerable costs entailed in his declaration to the commission on his loss of voting rights. TsGA SPB. F. 9133. Op. 1. D. 23. L.17. Zaiavlenie Vladimira Bogacheva v pushkinskuiu gorodskuiu komissiiu po delam lisheniia izbiratel'nykh prav, December 20, 1930.

[63] Viacheslav Iakovlevich Shishkov (1873–1945) was a Soviet writer and author of the novel *Ugrium-Reka*. From 1927, Shishkov lived in Detskoe Selo. Late in 1927, the Bolsheviks began a campaign against the owners of private apartments on the pretext of mounting a struggle against the housing crisis. Everyone who had more than eight square meters of living space per person was obliged to "increase their housing density," that is, to admit residents of their choice. When the lease ran out, the question of who moved in came to be decided by the regional authorities. Lebina, *Sovetskaia povsednevnost'*, 103–4.

[64] Aleksei Nikolaevich Tolstoi (1883–1945) was a Soviet writer from the Tolstoi extended family, known among other reasons for his return from emigration. He was a prominent functionary.

[65] Oskar Iur'evich Klever (1887–1975) was one of the members of the old Tsarskoe Selo intelligentsia, an artist and illustrator of the tales of Hans Christian Andersen. In February 1942, he was evacuated by the Germans, later returning to the USSR. Osipova indeed mentions him in a note from November 4: "The artist Klever ... was poisoned with tannin, and his legs were paralyzed. He needed milk. In the courtyard of the building where they lived, there was a woman who had a cow. Klever's sister went down on her knees and begged the woman to sell milk to her, but the woman refused, since she could get food from the Germans while money was of no use to her. One or another of the indignant neighbors called out to a passing German soldier, and told him the whole story. The German promptly beat the woman up, and ordered her to hand over the whole yield of milk for a week to the Klevers, free of charge. The Klevers took only as much as they needed, and paid the woman." Tsypin, *Gorod Pushkin v gody voiny*, 197–99; Budnitskii and Zelenina, *"Svershilos'. Prishli nemtsy!,"* 90.

This woman was genuinely comical. She lived together with her husband in the basement of No. 7, a place that was as sturdy as a bomb shelter, after moving there from her janitor's quarters (three rooms and a kitchen—the doctors envied her), and did not give milk to anyone apart from me and "Olga Ivanovna," since she was saving up cottage cheese and butter for her grandson, who had left with his mother for Leningrad. She was anticipating that before long the Germans "must" take Leningrad, that her daughter Shura would arrive with the grandson, and that there would be nothing to eat. She and her husband went hungry at the same time as they had butter, cottage cheese, milk, and also two *puds*[66] of white flour, several pounds of cocoa, sugar, and a box of Moskva"[67]* chocolates. Her husband, Fedor Kuz'mich, a wonderful man and devoted to his family, died from an intestinal obstruction after eating, at one sitting, a whole loaf of poor-quality bread that he had obtained when starting a job.[68]

Hundreds of people rushed to take such jobs in the knitwear factory, regarding the place as a kind of paradise where they could obtain a ration and where the physical work was not demanding.[69] My husband[70] had been appointed to the post of director, and people besieged him day and night, pleading with him to take them on. It was good that it was possible and necessary to choose women who were "specialists" on the knitting machines, otherwise people would have casually claimed that in order to be hired, one had to pay a bribe, that is, give back a weekly ration. Though thank God, my husband succeeded in living through the occupation, and no-one, either Russian or German,[71] ever looked at him askance. He managed a workplace with a crowd of 300 hungry

---

[66] *Pud* (pood) is a traditional Russian measure of weight: one *pud* equals approximately 16.38 kilograms (36.11 pounds).

[67] * Note by Baskakova: *They obtained all these goods through spontaneous robberies, after September 15, of the shops of the Gostinyi Dvor.*

[68] The "Evacuation" database, dedicated to evacuated citizens of Leningrad, lists Fedor Kuz'mich Rogach and three members of his family who had been living in Pushkin at 7 Moskovskaia Ulitsa. To judge from the evidence, only two actually managed to leave. Electronic database "Evakuatsiia" (https://evacuation.spbarchives.ru/). With reference to: TsGA SPB. F. 8557. Op. 6. D. 1020. L. 198.

[69] Supplies of warm winter clothing very quickly became vitally important to the Wehrmacht. Along with the massive requisitioning of goods from the local population (or to put it more simply, plunder), the German authorities also organized production. In the knitwear factory in Pavlovsk during the winter of 1941–1942, some 40 sweaters and 450 balaclavas were produced by hand each day. BArch Freiburg, RW 31/948. WiKdo Krasnogwardeisk, Lagebericht vom 10.1.42. We thank Dr. Jeff Rutherford for sharing this information with us.

[70] As one of the workers stated, "the knitwear factory was headed by Bogachev, who treated the workers well." Ivanova, *Za blokadnym kol'tsom*, 565.

[71] In the testimonies that were gathered from local residents by the Soviet commission charged with investigating German crimes (ChGK), Bogachev was counterposed to Sokovnin, the director of the mechanical workshops. The latter was considered to have treated workers badly.

people. Since he knew that Fedor Kuz'mich had food to eat, my husband refused to hire him for a long time, but then, after growing weary of the endless pleading, he took him on . . .

The fate of the cow was as follows. Eternally fearful for its safety, Fekla Grigor'evna and her husband decided to move it . . . into the basement, next to themselves, which they succeeded in doing. It was very comical to see the cow standing in the room. The soldiers did not give up and continued investigating.[72] Then Fekla and her husband decided the cow should be slaughtered. They invited a butcher whom they knew and the beautiful animal, which had a poetic name from mythology (I've tried to remember it, but I can't), perished in the cellars not of the Lubianka but of 7 Moskovskaia Ulitsa.

Above this cellar was the apartment of Viacheslav Shishkov, wrecked and plundered, with shelves full of books, trunks full of manuscripts and all sorts of papers torn apart, and with papers scattered throughout the entire premises. Out of all this wealth I took for myself a copy of Makarov's Russian-German dictionary with an inscription by Shishkov's wife, Kseniia Mikhailovna. This dictionary came with me to Australia.

Fekla Grigor'evna again began weeping, and asked for help with removing the meat and hiding it so that the Germans would not take it. Here, Sister Bednova came to her aid, deciding to take the carcass out bit by bit on a sled, wrapped in a quilted blanket, like a patient.

Somehow it was not frightening, but jolly and adventurous—slowly, sedately stepping in felt boots through the deep snow of the garden, accompanying the "patient" and pulling another sled with the belongings of this "patient," consisting of a mattress and pillows. We went through the whole city with Red Cross armbands on our sleeves, a doctor and nurse heading in the direction of the hospital. But on the boulevard, we turned abruptly toward the Moscow Gates, next to which there always stood a soldier with the breastplate of the *Feldgendarmerie*[73] on his chest, and who usually knew that we lived there. If he did not know this, we showed him our *Bescheinigung*.[74]

---

[72] Compare this with the diary of Ivanov-Razumnik: "22.01 Episode with two Germans and Fekla Rogach's cow. 23.01: During the night the Germans are said to have taken away Rogach's cow. – Fekla Rogach asked Varia to stay overnight with her until 24/1. The Germans arrived. A triple interrogation of Rogachik. Varia as official *Dolmetscher*! [interpreter]." Amherst College/The Ivanov-Razumnik diary. Entries from January 22 and 23, 1942.

[73] Field gendarmes, the military police of the Wehrmacht.

[74] Permission, pass (*German*).

We had *always*[75] lived on Moskovskoe Shosse, in building No. 15, and when this burnt down, Ol'ga Ivanovna [Videman] invited us to live with her in No. 21. We had long been acquainted with her, and she had often given German language lessons to our son. After a while it became clear that the Germans she kept company with were not to our liking; there was an eternal crowd of young and not-so-young German men, paying court both to her and to her two charming daughters, fifteen-year-old Ol'ia and seventeen-year-old Zhenia. Dances, a gramophone and piano, and . . . endless food. It would have been bearable, if she had not done her utmost to drag us into this *as well*.[76]

If a guest was older and held a high rank, she would play the card of my husband's origins in the nobility, of the fact that he was an engineer, had his own car, was well versed in music and books, and owned a marvelous, rare copy of Benois's book "Tsarskoe Selo." On one occasion, the commandant[77]* asked to read this book for a little while (it was in French), and for a long time did not return it. Finally, my husband grew tired of asking Ol'ga Ivanovna, and went personally to the commandant, especially since a transfer was due to take place, and it would be the turn of the Austrians to manage the city.[78] And what then? The commandant returned the book, neatly wrapped up and with his thanks. Ol'ga Ivanovna twittered delightedly that the Germans were such good, refined people, and that there was no reason to fear for the book's safety. Unfolding the wrapper, my husband saw a completely different volume, badly tattered, without a single drawing . . . everything had been torn out.

The volume was from the book repository of the palace, where the Germans rummaged about unendingly. Among other things, they removed the wonderful tiles from Dutch stoves of the time of Peter the Great and brought them to the workshop of the mechanical plant to be set in a frame.[79] Applying himself earnestly to this art, and demonstrating great talent, was a worker named Sorokin, who of course received from the Germans miserable portions of *Honig*, *Käse*, and *Mehl*,[80] and . . . most importantly, bread, or to be more accurate, gnawed-at scraps of it.

---

[75] Word in italics is crossed out in the original text.

[76] Words in italics are crossed out in the original text.

[77] Note by Baskakova: *The commandant at that time was a "pastor" by profession.*

[78] On April 30, 1942, the 121st Infantry Division, occupying Pushkin, handed over its sector to the 5th Mountain Division from Salzburg. One of the residents recalled that "the fascist units in the city were replaced by Austrians with edelweiss on their headgear." Tsypin, *Gorod Pushkin v gody voiny*, 142.

[79] The mechanical workshops, the knitwear factory, and the felting works were the only enterprises operating in Pushkin and Pavlovsk under the Germans.

[80] Honey, cheese, flour (*German*).

After all, the German soldier was always half-starved himself. This was especially apparent when the Spanish Blue Division,[81] with its abundance of food provisions, arrived in Pushkin, and when the Germans, who despised and hated the Spaniards, began quietly visiting the Spanish kitchens, concealing this from their commanders and from one another. In these kitchens were vats of soup made from beans and a multitude of finely cut pieces of fatty pork. The soup was so thick that, it was said, you could not stir it with a spoon. Dear God! What a golden time began, too, for us starving civilians who had unfortunately remained in very small numbers in the city of Pushkin.

The whole population (one and a half thousand) had been concentrated by the Germans at two points, not counting, of course, the small groups of workers, mainly young, who served the German units and who lived there.[82] One of these points was a huge building of three stories, occupying an entire block, in which police had lived in tsarist times, and which more recently had been the student hostel of the Agricultural Institute.[83] By the time the Blue Division arrived, the people who were living (or who were concentrated) in this building were the workers serving the mechanical works and its departments, along with their families.

It was a real barracks situation. Early in the morning life began with the blowing of a whistle and a shout from "crazy Peter"—the assistant of the equally crazy and harsh Edenhardt,[84] *Sonderführer* of the mechanical plant—"Wasser holen!"[85] The locked doors that led onto the street were opened, and a file of men, women, and children armed with buckets emerged and went to the park, to the pond. Returning home, the people soon used this water to make soup for themselves in a common kitchen, a very large space with a huge stove that had been built by the workers themselves.

In this same space, I remember, concerts by an amateur group were held twice in the presence of the higher-ups, and in this very kitchen a Spanish

---

[81] The 250th Infantry Division (the Spanish Blue Division) entered Pushkin in the first week of September 1942.

[82] The last sizeable evacuation from Pushkin and Pavlovsk was conducted on the orders of the 50th Corps from the sixth to the fourteenth of August 1942, on the eve of the arrival of the Spanish legionaries. The only residents who were left were workers in the factories, who were rehoused in ghettoes, and medical personnel. According to German data, some 869 people remained in Pushkin. Rutherford, *Combat and Genocide on the Eastern Front*, 288.

[83] The residential building of the Palace Administration, on the corner of Sredniaia Ulitsa and Tserkovnaia Ulitsa.

[84] Mentioned in a report: BArch Freiburg, RW 31/948, WiKdo Krasnogwardeisk, Monatsbericht Februar 1942, February 26, 1942.

[85] Get water! (*German*).

soldier who had jumped in through a window (the kitchen was on the ground floor) to light up, and who had plied the workers with cigarettes, was mortally wounded by Peter. Sister Bednova, who had been close by, tried to render first aid to the wounded man by stopping his blood loss. She bound up his thigh with a towel, which was, however, not enough, and when she tried to undo the soldier's belt to use it for the same purpose, Peter dealt her a string of slaps in the face and drove her out of the room. At the noise the Spaniards came running, Peter disappeared, and the wounded man was carried out. Later, it was learned that he had died. Peter was handed over to a German court, and in sum, went off on *Urlaub*[86] to his homeland.

In winter, the working day began at 8 a.m. Again, the doors were opened, and when the whistle sounded, the workers came out in two groups, escorted by soldiers. After proceeding a short distance, one group turned and headed toward the mechanical works, while the other made for the former imperial garages, which were located just a kilometer from the front line.[87]

The work in these garages was overseen by my husband, who was an automotive engineer; he used to say that from the roof you could see the Russians moving about in their trenches. In the hostel, we were given an apartment of three rooms and a kitchen. Occupying a similar apartment, but on the other corner of the building, was another engineer, V. V. Sokovnin, and his wife.[88]

The windows of our apartment looked out onto the Pushkin Gardens and the Znamenie Church. In the Pushkin Gardens there were trenches and shell-holes that later were filled with corpses. The part of the building where our apartment was located was outside the line of fire coming from the Russians, and that was why we moved in there. Sokovnin, meanwhile, was scornful of precautions of this kind. Of course, it was difficult to hide in these circumstances, and shells, not small ones, and more often incendiary bombs, fell on our building from all directions. Once, a huge shell hit right on the wall of Sokovnin's apartment, tore the cast-iron central heating radiator from beneath the window, and flung it onto the bottom edge of his bed (Sokovnin would later relate that he had still been asleep, and had just turned to the wall and drawn his legs up; as a result, he received only a small bruise to his feet). Later, a shell penetrated obliquely

---

[86]   Leave (*German*).

[87]   The mechanical works were located on Ulitsa Novoderevenskaia to the east of the railway station, while the imperial garages were next to the Fedorovskii village on Ulitsa Akademicheskaia. The line of the front was, indeed, practically next door.

[88]   Vasilii Vasil'evich Sokovnin (1900–?) lived at 14 Ulitsa Kommunarov, together with three members of his family. He was later evacuated to Germany, and his subsequent fate is unknown. TsGA SPB. F. 5557. Op. 6. D. 1020. L. 409. Akty-spiski naseleniia g. Pushkin, 1944g.

through several premises and exploded on the third floor in the room of an independent worker, a first-rate tailor of outer garments, Volkov. A few pieces of his body were gathered together in a box and buried, also in the Pushkin Gardens. To dig a separate grave, it would have been necessary to spend a long time thawing out the earth with a fire. One of his hands was found gripped tightly on a piece of caracal fur. He had been working on this piece early in the morning before leaving for the factory. Many residents suffered at that time from shell fragments and from the bricks falling from wrecked walls.

Survival above all: Winter-Spring 1942

From September 1942 to March 1943, we lived in our apartment, which was comfortable despite everything. We were surrounded by three hundred well-wishing people who for the most part were either my patients or the spiritual patients of my husband, who oversaw the work in the garage. There he had his own *Sonderführer*, separate from the mechanical works, a wonderful, kind German named Strauss who spent much of his working day taking walks about the dead city and collecting various small things that he could post in a two-kilogram package to his wife in Germany. Examples of what he collected were: pieces of Morocco and other kinds of leather that he cut off neatly from the binding of books and albums; frames for portraits and small pictures; and other things. He brought everything back and showed it to my husband.

Once he brought a frame and cut out of it . . . a marvelous drawing by Ostroumova-Lebedeva,[89] a view of St. Petersburg, with the Neva enveloped in mist, the Petropavlovskaia Fortress, barges on the river, and the edge of the granite parapet of the embankment. My husband explained everything to him, but he said that this did not interest him, and pinned the picture to the wall in his office. For some reason Edenhardt came by, and saw it on the wall. Realizing that it was Leningrad, he took out his revolver and fired two bullets into it, saying: "We'll soon be there ourselves."

This was a good time mainly because of the presence of the Spaniards, who sharply improved the nutrition of the remaining handful of the population.

---

[89] Anna Petrovna Ostroumova-Lebedeva (1871–1955) was a St. Petersburg and Leningrad artist and a highly skilled engraver. During the period that Baskakova describes, she was on the other side of the blockade ring, in Leningrad, and created a series of drawings with views of the besieged city. She left diaries that have been published in part. "Anna Petrovna Ostroumova-Lebedeva (1871–1957)," in *Writing the Siege of Leningrad: Women's Diaries, Memoirs, and Documentary Prose*, ed. Jonathan Harris (Pittsburgh, PA: University of Pittsburgh Press, 2002), 25–32.

By nature very good-hearted, they would push cigarettes and canned foods on the men and sweets on the women, without recompense and even without being asked. By that time no-one possessed jewelry any longer, and the Spaniards did not ask for it. Where they were concerned, the main currency was icons—the most commonplace Orthodox icons, in metal mountings or without them, and especially depictions of the Mother of God. These were present in abundance. If there were not enough icons within the walls of the hostel, and the demand was present, then there were sources that could be turned to—Sister Bednova, for example. The two of us had only one permanent pass (I kept it on me) for going to the hospital, which was located in Sofiia,[90] not far from the Kochubei Palace, where the rest of the population lived and where the German command was quartered.

The pass, of course, specified a certain route, but this did not trouble Bednova, and she went fearlessly down side streets, since along the line of the route there were parks that spread off to the right, and along the edge of the parks, by the canal that led from the "Swan," lay the cemetery for SS soldiers,[91] while to the left stood the blackened walls of the Milk Institute.[92] While passing by the ruins of this beautiful building, the former imperial orangeries, I once saw pillars of smoke and tongues of flame coming from the cellars. I looked in through one of the holes in the wall and beheld the following phantasmagoric picture: in the middle of the empty space was an open fire, hanging over which was a large cauldron full of boiling oil (as I then imagined), and a crowd of smoke-blackened, scruffy-looking Spaniards were throwing pieces of toasted bread into the cauldron and taking them out again. Against the background of the bright flames of the fire these jumping figures resembled devils. What was unusual was the quiet in the cellar (they were busy with their food), since the Spaniards are a very vocal people.[93]

---

[90] The southern part of the city of Pushkin around the Sofiiskii Cathedral, founded in the eighteenth century by Catherine II as a separate town and later incorporated into Tsarskoe Selo.

[91] In September 1941, Pushkin was taken by the SS Police Division as part of the 50th Army Corps. Later, the SS soldiers were positioned in and around the city. There are well-known photos, taken by David Trachtenberg in 1944, of birch crosses next to the Ekaterininskii Palace. Tsypin, *Gorod Pushkin v gody voiny*, 262–63.

[92] The "Swan" fountain and the Orangeries building, which housed the Institute of the Refrigeration and Milk Industry.

[93] The same was recalled by Osipova, who on September 17, 1942, wrote in her diary: "My captain, as happy as if he had received a gift, shouted and ran about the yard. The soldiers too yelled and ran about no less than he did, all of them smeared with clay, like devils. Seeing my laundresses, the captain began shouting frantically to the soldiers, telling them to go and help. Incidentally, the Spaniards in all their experiences yell as if they were being slaughtered. They experience everything very acutely and passionately, so that there is an incessant uproar over the city suggesting

They did not notice me, or else they would certainly have invited me to "share their table," and I beat a quick retreat, since I was always afraid of face-to-face meetings. After all, the Spanish soldier is just as much a rapist as the German, with the sole difference that if the woman or girl puts up the slightest resistance, he leaves her be, without doing anything to her, while the German soldier is a one-hundred-percent rapist. Once he has seized his victim, he never lets her out of his hands, and afterwards—afterwards he shoots her. This is explained by the fact that the German soldier is subject to strict discipline, and answers to a military court. The Spanish army is very lax, and the soldiers are not afraid of their commanders.

Let me give some examples. During the first months of the German occupation, victims were twice brought to us in the polyclinic (at that time, it was still in its usual home at 13 Moskovskaia Ulitsa). I remember that one of them was a twelve-year-old girl with a gag in her mouth, blue and unconscious. She soon died. The other was a woman with her hands bound and also with a gag, half-dead from fear and exhaustion. She survived. The German command did not even search for the perpetrators, since both victims had been living in a so-called forbidden zone.

After the Germans entered Pushkin the commandant from time-to-time placed bans on various regions of the city, on various streets, and even on particular sides of the streets. This was explained as being for military reasons—the disposition of units, and the locations of gun emplacements and mines. Among the population there were many people who did not submit to this, and who did not abandon their familiar places. For some, this might be because of hoards of food they had buried (half a barrel of cabbages, or a sack of cabbages). Meanwhile, beneath the snow, there were cabbage stalks in the vegetable gardens. The people were so weak that they would not go beyond their dwellings, and thus remained unnoticed.

In the spring, when the stench rose from the rotting corpses of these "deviants," the commandant ordered the city administration to equip a sanitary team under the direction of Dr. B., a neuropathologist (?!?) (later, he contrived to pass himself off as a German and to leave for Germany).[94] This team

---

the end of the world. The population used to get alarmed, but now they are used to it." Budnitskii and Zelenina, "Svershilos'. Prishli nemtsy!," 141.

[94] Supposedly, this is Dr. Petr Vladimirovich Baranovskii. According to the Soviet population lists from 1944, there was a man with this name who resided in Pushkin before the war, in a family of three. Ivanov-Razumnik mentioned in his notebook a certain "Dr. Baranovskii," who was evacuated to Germany slightly later than him; this doctor wrote a letter describing the situation in Pushkin. In 1949, a medical doctor named Petr Vladimirovich Baranovskii, along with his wife

consisted of militia members[95] harnessed to sleds and carts, who went about the "city of the dead" loading their vehicles with corpses, while unloading the dead of the "superfluous weight" of any valuables that might be on their bodies beforehand. A disagreeable job became somewhat more attractive as a result, and hence there were numerous men, unsqueamish and not easily put off, who sought to join the militia.

But let me return to the question of rape. Later, in the winter of 1942, Gospozha L., a worker in the knitwear factory, came to the polyclinic, which by this time was housed in the Sofiia region on Ulitsa Krasnoi Zvezdy. Leaving the factory in the twilight, she was set upon by two Spaniards, who seized her and threw her onto the snow. Humorously and without rancor, L. related to us how for a lengthy period they had toiled over her, ineffectually, since she was thoroughly rugged up because of the deep frost. And she also said, laughing, "I must be completely overgrown by now, I've been a widow for ages." Lying in the snow and calling for help, she was picked up by Peter, who was going by in a car, and was taken home. The Spaniards made off, cursing.

I also remember another elderly woman from a village near Pushkin, who was raped by three Spanish soldiers. She suffered a fractured and dislocated shoulder, and fractured ribs. They did not shoot her, and she eventually recovered. After attending to her I returned in the company of my dear, unforgettable surgical sister Fokina, pulling a sled loaded with cabbages and swedes, and also with a canister of milk.

Irina and their two sons, emigrated to Australia. He was registered as a "Lithuanian," who lived in Kaunas; however, in one of the documents, his son Vladimir's place of birth in 1937 is listed as "Buskin" (clearly, "Pushkin" was the true place). We are not completely confident that Baskakova's doctor and the Australian one are one and the same person. Irina, his wife, was born Mallein in Petrograd in 1917, a descendant of the famous architect and engineer Nikolai Mallein, who in 1920 had designed the first Russian crematorium. In 1925, Irina resided with her father in Leningrad. The Australian neuropathologist Peter Baranowsky penned a number of books, such as *Living with a Bad Back* and *How to Live Longer, Look Younger and Slow Down Old Age*. Baranowsky died in 1997 in Albany City, effectively outliving the Bolshevik dictatorship that had messed up his life. TsGA SPB. F. 8557. Op. 6. D. 388. Spiski naseleniia (Pushkin); Amherst College/The Ivanov-Razumnik diary. Entry from March 31, 1942; Online Archive of the Bad Arolsen Archives. Postwar Card File. Reference code 03010101. AEF DP Registration record No. D1052475, March 16, 1946; AEF DP Registration Record, Document No. 66503809, October 15, 1948; Lists of all persons of United Nations and other foreigners, German Jews and stateless persons; American Zone; Bavaria, Hesse (1) Reference Code DE ITS 2.1.1.1 BY 067 LIT ZM, document no. 69958764; TsGA SPB. F. 3178. Op. 13. D. 1144. L. 9. Anketnyi list N. I. Malein, 1925; https://www.findagrave.com/memorial/179601370/peter-baranowski.

95   In Pushkin, this familiar term, which had previously designated the Soviet police, most likely referred to the auxiliary Russian police force that had been set up by the Germans and was subject to the city authorities. Ivanov-Razumnik recorded in his notebook: "The militia are idlers and swindlers, despised by the entire population." Amherst College/The Ivanov-Razumnik diary. Entry from January 9, 1942.

Our young women were more willing to enter the "service" of the Spaniards than of the Germans, which roused the latter to fury. The Germans even distributed leaflets among young people warning of the savageries with which the barbaric Spaniards threatened them. This was of no use, and many women retained favorable memories of the Spaniards. Some even left for Spain with them, for example, the Neverovskii family whom I knew well—a grandmother and a mother with three daughters.[96]

Yes, the Spaniards made off, leaving both women alive, but a German would have acted differently, as happened in Pushkin during the winter of 1942, I forget in which month. The rape victim was a young woman, the physician Elena Matskevich. She was supporting a young daughter and her aged parents, who needed to be fed, but how? Reasoning that the Germans would provide nothing to medical workers who were not serving them but were only looking after the civilian population (the Germans began providing us with a miserable ration only in March 1942), she secured work in the kitchen of one of the German units. She told me that she was in a good situation, since she herself had plenty to eat, and she was bringing enough food home. There was just one particularly dangerous area of the front near the railway station, which was often shelled, and returning home by way of the forbidden zone of the boulevard was not without its perils. Nevertheless, the commanders and soldiers treated her well; she had some success in communicating with them in Russian, while at the same time studying German. She even conducted anti-Bolshevist propaganda, since among the Germans were people who were highly sympathetic to those ideas. Hence, Dr. Matskevich revealed our Bolshevist reality to them.

Every evening when she returned home, a soldier accompanied her. She worked in the kitchen for several months, and did not abandon it even when the commandant granted her permission to open a private surgery in her apartment, and to practice among the civilian population.

I do not know whether she had earlier been a specialist gynecologist, but I had seen that she had surgical skills on that nightmarish night within the walls of the hospital, when she and I worked at adjoining tables. At any rate, she soon acquired a clientele among our women and girls, serving the Germans not just for a piece of bread and a potful of peas, but also for silk stockings (the market price of which was two pounds of butter) and other enticing

---

[96] No Neverovskii family could be found in the lists of residents of the city. The family may have had another, similar surname, Neviarovich or Nemirovskii.

goods. For performing an operation, she charged them in food: a pound of but-ter, ten pounds of white flour, or something else.

She was regarded as very expensive, and of course there was no point in women applying to her who were hungry and ragged, and had "fallen ill" un-expectedly, by chance. Such women did not go to the hospital either, since such operations were not supposed to be performed there, and women finished up there only when suffering from hemorrhages after failed attempts at self-help. As doctors, we took a very disapproving attitude to the medical activity of Dr. Matskevich, though some of us did not conceal the fact that we envied her suc-cesses in obtaining food. One such person was Dr. Levanevskaia (according to Osipova's transcription, Paderevskaia),[97] who after Matskevich's death, and after we were all evacuated in March 1943, became the owner of the whole ex-pensive set of gynecological instruments that Lelia Matskevich had possessed. Personally, I can say that Lelia operated on me twice at my request, and abso-lutely without charge.

Witnessing: A visit to the POW camp and Dr. Matskevich's fate

On one occasion, however, I had the chance to help her "earn" such luxury items as cocoa, chocolate, and two pairs of underwear. Dr. Savel'eva[98] and I were or-dered, just once, to visit a prisoner-of-war camp in the automobile park. We were warmly dressed, and as I remember, found it agreeable walking through the crunching snow on a clear frosty day. Of course, we were chewing on cakes we had grabbed, made of bran and beets and very similar in appearance to un-cooked rissoles. Their deceptive appearance once misled me, when in some-one's house I was treated to similar rissoles, and I could not conceal my hun-gry disappointment; this greatly offended my host, who was very proud of his command of the culinary arts. I learned the ways of his culinary art, but my hunger did not abate.

We arrived at the barracks premises of the "precinct," which were very clean and cold. The commandant immediately summoned us. We appeared before

---

[97]   Once again, pseudonyms are involved. Poliakova-Osipova in her writings devoted a good many angry lines to the doctors, and especially to Bednova and Paderevskaia-Levanevskaia. In a note on December 2, 1941, she exclaimed: "People like Paderevskaia, Bednova, and Korovin [Dr. Ur-taev] stole everything." Budnitskii and Zelenina, *"Svershilos'. Prishli nemtsy!,"* 99.

[98]   This may refer to Anna Karlovna Savel'eva, a doctor at the polyclinic. Z. Polosukhina, "Uchitel'nitsa," *Bol'shevistskoe Slovo,* no. 35, March 25, 1941, 3; TsGA SPB. F. 8557. Op. 6. D. 1020. L. 364. Akti-spis-ki zhitelei g. Pushkin, 1944g.

him, ruddy from the frost, animated, and beautifully dressed in furs; I was even wearing a white arctic fox fur that had been saved from the fire, and which together with other soft items of outer clothing had served me as a pillow during a month spent sitting in a bomb shelter. The commandant's stern eyes softened, and he began talking with us quite kindly. He instructed us in his sanitary measures, and asked us to examine sick men who were suspected of having typhus (according to him, they were shirkers who were unwilling to go out and work).

The commandant graciously invited Dr. Savel'eva and me to have lunch with him after we had examined the patients. We left him with unflappable faces, but his last words aroused a storm of delight in our hearts and stomachs. We spent two hours performing the examinations. Helping us was a *lekpom*[99] from among the prisoners of war, a man named Rumiantsev, cheerful and efficient, with a wide knowledge of medical matters, and with a great store of concern for the men under his care. At the outset we enquired of him whether we could speak openly with him in Russian, that is, whether any of the Germans surrounding us understood the Russian language. He reassured us in that regard, and we then proceeded to examine two or three dozen men who had been selected on suspicion of having typhus.

In our view, all of these were men in the middle stage of exhaustion from malnutrition. No more than two or three had typhus, though this was more than enough to place all the prisoners in this camp at risk, and thus for almost all of those presented for examination to be categorized without hesitation as "suspected." Both the patients and the feldsher Rumiantsev were very satisfied with our conclusion, since they supposed that in Gatchina, where the men would be sent, they would be better fed and would, of course, recover. I should note that these illusions soon vanished. We were to learn of the next act of inhumanity of the Germans, who set fire to a similar hospital containing a thousand people, and when these people tried to crawl out of all the gaps in the fence, shoved them back inside.[100]

I remember that Rumiantsev was to fall sick later, and it was with difficulty that I managed to have him placed in our hospital, where there was a typhus section, after gaining the permission of the camp commanders and also our Pushkin commandant.

---

[99] A medical assistant, a feldsher.

[100] According to testimonies by witnesses, in Gatchina in 1941, a typhus barracks was burnt along with prisoners of war. Some 170 people died. GARF. F. R-7021. Op. 30. D. 241. L. 10. Akt Gatchinskoi gorodskoi komissii ChGK o zlodeianiiakh nemetsko-fashistskikh zakhvatchikhov v g. Gatchina Leningradskoi oblasti v period okkupatsii, 24.11.1944.

After we had examined the patients, we asked to be allowed to inspect the premises. We were shown a spacious barracks with two tiers of bunks, devoid of any sign of bedding but also, it must be acknowledged, of any sign of bedbugs. Nevertheless, the lice—the main vectors of typhus—had gone off to work together with their hosts and their hosts' ragged clothes. Both the floor and the bunks were wet after being swabbed and stank unbearably of carbolic. Rumiantsev stated that this was done daily, and that it led to many colds and cases of pneumonia, since the wet prisoners were lying on wet planks that had not been able to dry out because of the lack of heating.

The death rate in the camp was very high. The prisoners themselves barely spoke with us, and gave only brief answers to our questions concerning their ailments. They had been trained by their fear of beatings and hunger. The camp at that time produced a terrifying impression on me of my own hopeless situation. I had, of course, never spent time in Soviet concentration camps.

We returned to the commandant with lowered heads, having now lost our joy in life. We told him of our thoughts and impressions concerning the sanitary measures. None of this was new to him, since he had already had such a conversation with Dr. Urtaev (the same Korovin), who had drawn up plans for a primitive method of delousing. Savel'eva and I, lacking faith in the talents of Urtaev, tried to persuade the commandant to turn to the German medical units for such a system. The commandant of course rejected our advice, and later, we had cause repeatedly to be convinced of our correctness. Dr. Urtaev's delousing system, which he advertised both in Russian and German circles, failed dismally, but despite this, Urtaev himself was raised to the title of burgomaster after Zolotukhin left this post.[101]

When the official discussions had ended, lunch began, and the conversations took on a private and even deeply personal nature. I distinctly remember a dish with steaming potatoes, surrounded by a pile of exquisitely prepared "beef stroganoff." All this wealth was provided to us two, while the commandant merely sipped wine, and offered it to us as well. Savel'eva declined it, because she was breast-feeding her now two-year-old child, while I drank only one glass, since such things were not to my liking. Nevertheless, I asked the

---

[101] Prior to the war, Vasilii Nikanorovich Zolotukhin had been a school inspector. On April 6, 1942, he was appointed burgomaster of Pavlovsk. In the recollections of witnesses the sequence and order of the appointment of Russian burgomasters differs. Lidiia Mikhailovna Klein-Burzi, who personally worked in the administration, recalled that the first head of the city government was Urtaev, who was replaced in November 1941 by Zolotukhin, and that it was only in the summer of 1942 that Seleznev was appointed. Petr Mansurov noted that "in December 1941, they replaced the burgomaster Urtaev." Ivanova, *Za blokadnym kol'tsom*, 561.

commandant if some bread, which was completely lacking, could be brought to the table, and this was done. I do not remember whether anything remained on the dish, but of the loaf of bread fully half remained. Ignoring the commandant, we gazed hungrily at it, but our host did not deign to offer it to us.

The table-talk ranged over various topics, even including political ones. I remember that this was the first time I had heard the expression, "German national socialism is not for export."[102] At that time, we Russians often thought about the reconstruction of life after the power of the Bolsheviks was overthrown, imagining it along the lines of German national socialism, though of course without the "Führer." But since for the present it was not Russians but Germans who were overthrowing the Bolsheviks, then whether we liked it or not, it was the "Führer" who was an eyesore to us. Reconstruction was still a long way off, and for the time being we had to live and help others to live.

After lunch the commandant asked me, on my own, to go with him into the next room. It turned out that he wanted me to look at his "girl," to determine whether she was pregnant. He himself went out, and into the room came a pretty, not particularly young woman. We talked for a little, and it turned out that she knew me as having been a member of the city soviet for the 17th district, where she lived. She had had dealings with me when I had tried, quite unsuccessfully, to get her the materials for a stove and for the roof of her house.[103]

The two of us spent perhaps fifteen minutes in agreeably amusing reminiscences, but after that I managed to determine that she was indeed pregnant. This discovery caused her no joy, and cast a pall over her mood from then on. She was very anxious for me, personally, to save her from "having a little German." I refused outright, since she knew perfectly well that I was not a gynecologist, and that in any case I did not have the instruments. Then I recalled Dr. Matskevich, and warmly recommended her. The commandant appeared, and everything was reported to him. He promptly sat everyone in a car, got behind the wheel himself, and took us to the address I indicated. Matskevich turned out not to be in the apartment, but with her "*Kompanie*."[104] Neverthe-

---

[102] "A rumor: the city administration *in corpore* applied for its members to be accepted into the national socialist organization. *Se non e vero*... [Even if it is not true, it is well conceived]." Amherst College/The Ivanov-Razumnik diary. Entry from January 4, 1942.

[103] In November 1939, Evdokiia Bogacheva had been elected as a deputy to the Pushkin Soviet of People's Deputies for the 92nd district. One of the most painful questions that arose constantly in the city newspaper and in the discussions between the deputies was that of house repairs. TsGA SPB. F. 4958. Op. 1. D. 32. L. 74, 75, 80. Stenograficheskii otchet zasedaniia Pushkinskogo raisoveta February 1, 1940.

[104] Military unit (*German*).

less, we agreed on the date for the operation with the doctor's mother, who acted as her assistant.

Subsequently, everything passed off successfully, to the complete satisfaction of both sides. Soon after that, Lelia Matskevich failed to return home from her *"Kompanie."* Nor did she appear the following day. Her father went to the commandant's office. Enquiries were directed to the unit where she worked; there, the answer was that she had left at her usual time, accompanied by a soldier. Questions were then asked of the policeman who had been on duty that day at the Moskovskii Gates. He affirmed that he had seen her in the company of a soldier who, as the policeman had often observed before, took his leave of her not far from the police post; Dr. Matskevich had then made her way alone along a short alley at the end of which stood the large building of the 1st School (formerly, a *Realschule*[105] in Tsarist times).

The policeman noted that at the same time two artillery soldiers had been walking through this alley. Dr. Matskevich's father walked around the empty buildings of the entire region, but discovered nothing. He also went into the school. After three days of futile searches the commandant himself decided to join in the effort. Then, accompanied by his assistant and the faithful Ol'ga Ivanovna, he also grabbed me for my medical expertise, since the Germans were well aware of what could be expected in such situations. Together with the father, we first began inspecting the huge premises that had suffered badly from shellfire back in August, September, and October, when more than two thousand people had huddled in its basements, which were very poorly suited for this purpose (we had piled the windows above ground level with library books and cabinets). Whichever corner I looked into, the father invariably said he had looked there already.

Finally, we went down to the first floor. There I entered a room in which I had been once before, when it had not been a classroom but an office. At that time I had been collecting the papers of my son, who had just completed his tenth class. Now, on this memorable day, there was a disorderly scene of school desks, with the floor covered in shell splinters and debris. The father kept telling me he had looked there already, and Ol'ga Ivanovna said that she and the commandant had done the same. They were about to leave the school.

My attention fell upon a large geographical map that was covering something. I approached, lifted the edge of the map, and saw the dead body of Lelia Matskevich. Ol'ga Ivanovna returned immediately with the commandant, and

---

[105] Real School (*German*), introduced in Russia during the reign of Nicholas I after the German school model, was a vocationally oriented type of secondary education, which trained its students for modern professional careers.

they began examining the scene. Matskevich lay on her back, dressed in her grey caracul jacket and a skirt of black cloth. Her right knee was bent; her skirt did not cover her legs, and her knickers were half pulled off. Next to her lay her empty leather handbag. Her head, in a fur cap, lay in a small pool of congealed blood, and bore the traces of a gunshot wound; in her right temple was a round hole, obviously the entry point of a revolver bullet, while in her left temple the opening was a little bigger. To the great displeasure of Herr Kommandant, I refused to supply an on-the-spot medical testimony.

Uttering cries of "Jammer, jammer!"[106] a handsome German who had appeared from somewhere ran about the room. Ol'ga Ivanovna said he was the head of the unit where Matskevich worked. I went home and put together for myself an approximate picture of the crime. As she walked toward the school, in the twilight and with no-one else around, Lelia was seized by the soldiers and forced through the doors of the school, which as I remember had always stood half-open. There they had dragged her into a nearby classroom, had evidently tried to persuade her to give her consent, and when she refused, had shot her, without trying to take her by force. The latter was indicated by the complete absence of any sign of a struggle and by the state of her clothing.

Later, her father said that in her handbag or on her wrist she was carrying a good-quality gold watch. That day she had also had money on her, 250 marks. Neither the one nor the other was still present. The Germans buried her solemnly, not placing her in a pit but taking her to a real cemetery. I bid farewell to her in her apartment. She was lying, looking as if she were alive, on the table on which she had been accustomed to carry out her operations.

That day her parents, almost on their knees, begged me to continue her work, and to give just a third of the proceeds to them and their granddaughter. I refused flat out. Their position was very difficult, but soon afterwards almost the entire population began to be evacuated, and Matskevich's family was resettled in Gatchina. Her instruments were sold for a very good price, while the Germans gave the parents and their granddaughter a small ration, no doubt in recognition of the services the daughter and mother had performed for the German command.

I should say that I do not condemn her. She was young, wanted to live, and not to let her child and parents die. She did not do a great deal of good for the Russian population, but nor did she intentionally do evil to anyone.

May she rest in peace.[107]

---

[106] Misery, misery! (*German*).

[107] Elena Vladimirovna Matskevich was killed on March 19, 1942. At the time of her death she was

"Poor people": Navigating between the different occupants

Subsequently, when we were living with the interpreter Videman and were acutely hungry, we gazed longingly in the direction of our burnt-out building, on the territory of which was buried the food that was so necessary to us. But the earth, iron-hard from the frost, did not yield to our miserable efforts. Finally, the long-awaited moment arrived, and we dug up our treasure. Everything was intact apart from some macaroni that had got wet. This we turned into dough, from which we made a kulich,[108] since Easter was approaching.

I remember well that our hoard consisted of 2 pounds of macaroni, two pounds of buckwheat meal, two pounds of wheat meal, two pounds of wheat, two pounds of granulated sugar, and four pounds of lard, which I obtained from a gravely ill man in the village of Kuz'mino, where the digging of trenches was then under way. From one minute to the next, noisy crowds of young people were running into the hut, either for water or looking for potatoes. The sick man refused outright to be admitted to hospital, saying, "It doesn't make any difference where you die from shellfire."

At home in Pushkin, our family were relatively well off for food, since I managed to sell a woman's fur coat to a Spanish general who closely resembled the Moor Othello. I bargained at length with his secretary Mavritsius[109] over the quantity of foodstuffs, and in the end, he supplied us each day with a certain part of the overall sum. He arrived on a highly unusual vehicle: a one-horse sleigh to which a large box, decorated in white, had been fitted. In this box sat Mavritsius, with butter, white flour, and canned meat that was bright red in color from an admixture of paprika. There was also tobacco (for others, since we did not smoke) and ten bottles of various wines and liqueurs. There were nuts

---

29 years old. Her family survived and remained on Soviet territory. Elena's stepfather, Leonid Odintsov, provided testimonies to the Soviet state commission on the investigation of German crimes. From these testimonies it emerges that Matskevich was a single mother and lived with her mother, her stepfather, and her son Vladimir. The father of Matskevich's child, Petr Iakovlevich Bogachenko, had been a surgeon in the Pavlovsk polyclinic before being called up to the Red Navy at the beginning of the war and serving in the Baltic. He took part in the catastrophic evacuation from Tallin on the ship *Andrei Zhdanov*, and finished the war as a lieutenant colonel in the medical service. In a declaration to the Soviet commission, Odintsov repeated his information about the stolen watch and money, and also stated that the rapists had been artillery soldiers.

108   Russian Orthodox Easter bread.

109   "Mavritsius" sounds completely unlike a Spanish name. Presumably it was a nickname thought up by Bogacheva for the adjutant of the "Moorish general," since the name Mauritius means "Moor." Who precisely of the officers of the Blue Division might have been imagined in the role of Othello is unclear.

of different kinds, halva, and sugared almonds. The negotiations with Mavritsius were conducted in French, which Spanish people in general often speak.

Mavritsius, it seemed to me, provided too little, while the Tatar speculators in Gatchina gave more. Grabbing my overcoat, I travelled to Gatchina in a "water mains" car. On the way we called in at Taitsy, at the main water supply point, and there we were almost killed. The Russians were firing on the locality, and the shells were being aimed very accurately. The car darted out of the line of fire and got away successfully.

Nothing worked out in the deal-making with the Tatars, which was good, since at home they were waiting for me, fearful that I would return without my overcoat (when I could have returned without my head). In my absence, the general himself had come with Mavritsius. On learning that I had gone to Gatchina to sell my overcoat, the general flew into a fearful rage, and as it seemed to my husband, began abusing Mavritsius for his stinginess (*pobre gente*).[110] Mavritsius translated these words in such a way that it seemed I could expect something close to death if this overcoat did not turn up. But to be brief, everything worked out, and in the end Mavritsius. . .

Once, managing to talk with him, I asked: "Is the general anxious to make a gift to his Desdemona?" To this, Mavritsius replied innocently that he thought the general's wife had a different name.

This family [the Neverovskiis] enjoyed respect and success among both the Germans and the Spaniards. Their behavior was very modest, despite the success of the mother and the two older girls. They were talented and played the piano well (their grandmother had taught them).[111] The girls performed in concerts for the commandant, always with a classical program, as well as providing the Germans with performances of light music and with their favorite clowning. The touching solicitude of the commandant toward them extended to the point where he displayed great willingness in granting permission to Sister Fokina and me to go and attend to patients, most often Finns, in nearby villages, knowing that as a doctor the population would give me food supplies and above all, milk. The Germans did not have milk at their disposal, and the commandant was most anxious to obtain it for the Neverovskii family's little daughter, Marisha, and also for 15-year-old Galia. The latter was very weak, de-

---

[110] Poor people (*Spanish*).

[111] Vitol'd Petrovich Pivovarun, who as an adolescent survived the occupation of Pushkin, recalled the Nemirovskii sisters performing in amateur concerts organized by the burgomaster Seleznev. Pivovarun, like Baskakova, spoke appreciatively of the concerts. Tsypin, *Gorod Pushkin v gody voiny*, 144.

spite the thoroughly satisfactory food supply that the family received from both the Germans and the Spaniards. I willingly shared with them the milk that we obtained and had brought back with difficulty (Fokina and I often came under fire), but did not give them anything else, since we were hungry enough ourselves, and it was also necessary to share with our comrades at work.

I would like to note here a streak of sentimentality that was present on the front line. The longing for the family hearth, consisting mainly of women and children, did not always have a sexual sub-plot. Nor did it have in this case. The apartment of the Neverovskii family was always open to visits both by the Germans and by the Spaniards, though not, of course, at the same time. It was not as noisy there as in our apartment with the interpreter Videman, where easy-going habits prevailed, and the Spaniards were absent. In the children's little room stood an open piano, from the depths of which the little fingers of the girls drew the wonderful sounds of the Russian and German classics. The Spaniards, who did not part with their guitars any more than with their automatics, sometimes brought a violin as well. It all worked very well, and the war was forgotten.

Where the guitars were concerned, I personally observed this picture. I was walking about the snow-covered city. Off in the distance a Spanish soldier was stringing a telephone line on the branches of the trees, and from time to time he would stop, leave his coil of wire and unfasten the guitar that was hanging on his back. Sad notes would then pour out into the clear, frosty air. For some reason the tones were almost always sad, although the Spanish soldiers themselves were a very cheerful lot, given to clowning about.

My husband related that to spite our German guards, the Spanish soldiers more than once accompanied a column of workers on their way to the plant, dancing, whistling, and playing on combs. The Spaniards, dressed in various women's rags on top of their uniforms, wore feathered hats on their heads and carried umbrellas in their hands. Some even rode children's bicycles. If the workers were going to the mechanical plant, where Edenhardt held sway, then in response to the shouting and whistling he would poke his head out the window, whereupon the Spaniards, heightening the uproar, would show him the *"lange Nase."*[112] Some who were especially bold ran up the stairs, and with a yell, slid down the banisters. This whole circus vanished instantly as soon as Edenhardt pulled out his pistol.

---

[112] Thumbing their nose (*German*).

The German officers hated the Spaniards, and the latter, aware of this, sought to enrage them however they could through clownish behavior. The Germans detested them still more because our young women were more willing to put themselves at the service of the Spaniards.

Of course, the surrounding people were not all convinced of the pure morals of the Neverovskii family, and even spoke of "a little brothel." But the people still liked them and did nothing to cause them harm.

The same cannot be said of the Videman family. It was openly said of them that the mother sold her daughters, which was not in fact the case. Our own family lived side by side with them for ten months, the hungriest and most frightening months of the German occupation for the entire population. Ol'ga Ivanovna Videman proved in fact to be very unpleasant, but after all, she was of German extraction (before the arrival of the Germans she came close to being jailed), and as a German, she served the German army sincerely and lovingly. She made a wonderful assistant to the commandants, observing military regulations meticulously, and every order issued by the commandant she considered the height of wisdom. For this reason, of course, she came into conflict with the population that complained through her to the commandant over the failure to obey these regulations. She was clever, cunning, and ... hungry. She had a good grasp of the needs and wishes of her superiors, and the population thus had a back door into her soul (and thank God that this back door existed).

She watched like a hawk over her girls, Zhenia and Ol'ia. On one occasion, Zhenia came running home from work (she cleaned the commandant's rooms) in tears and with a lock of hair pulled out of her scalp. She related that a soldier had tried to drag her into an empty building, and that she had barely managed to break free. After that the commandant ordered that she receive a permanent escort.

Both girls were light-minded, and like their mother, deaf to the miseries of others. Like their mother, they regarded it as perfectly natural that at the Moskovskii Gates a field gendarme, before the eyes of my husband, shot two women and two children who had come from the direction of Tiarlevo[113] with laden sleds—since, as the girls said, that was a forbidden zone, and the people were passing through it. My husband said later that he had tried, in his bad German, to explain to the gendarme that the people did not know about the order, since they had gone off to obtain food much earlier. Nevertheless, the gendarme took their passports, which amounted to a death sentence, and was supposed

---

[113] A settlement adjoining Pushkin on the south-east.

to hand the passports over to the commandant. My husband hurried away, but behind his back four gunshots rang out. Within the hour, Videman's girls came running home happily, dragging behind them a sled loaded with potatoes that the gendarme at the Moskovskii Gates had given them.

For a long time the bodies of the four people lay in a snowdrift, and a fifth was added to them. On my way home I saw a woman who turned out to be a patient of mine. I had managed with great difficulty and with a fictional diagnosis to have her admitted to the hospital, since she was dying of hunger and of a psychological disturbance after the death of her granddaughter in a children's home (to put starving people in the hospital without a specific illness was strictly forbidden). Seeing her, barely dragging her feet along, I ran to meet her and began trying to persuade her to return to the hospital, but she stubbornly repeated that her granddaughter had returned home, and that she was going to her. I explained to the gendarme that the woman was mad, grabbed her by the shoulders, turned her round, and gave her a push to try to get her to go back. She moved a few steps, and received a bullet in the back. It was the best outcome for her, but all the same it was hard, especially for a doctor, to watch the violent taking of a life.

Sometimes, too, it turned out that we could save such doomed people. This occurred twice. Somehow my husband happened to see the wife of one of his workers going along Moskovskoe Shosse with a sled, that is, past the building where we were living; she was heading, of course, toward the Moskovskii Gates and a gendarme's bullet. We intercepted her and took her back to our room, to the great annoyance of Ol'ga Ivanovna, who feared that harboring criminals would cause her to lose her reputation. Here, the potatoes helped. A few days later the "criminal" and the remaining potatoes were taken away in a car by my husband's wonderfully kind *Sonderführer*, Strauss.

The second case was very difficult for my husband, for me, and for our son, since we were asked to look out for the son of a woman worker returning [from the forbidden zone]. I remember how for several days the three of us took turns expecting the boy, who had not come on his own—there were four of them. To top everything off, they brought almost no food.

This time my husband had to exert pressure on Ol'ga Ivanovna psychologically, and not with potatoes. All these chances to aid the population, and also the possibility of exchanging various things for food with the Germans who visited the apartment, kept us living for a long time at 21 Moskovskoe Shosse. Also, Ol'ga Ivanovna was not anxious to have us leave, since she valued us highly, and counted on us. She knew that most of the population held us in good regard, and that if we shared her apartment, that meant she was not so bad. Nevertheless, we found the cramped space and endless noise irritating, and we persuaded her to ask the commandant to allow us to move to building No. 8 in the same forbidden zone, on the same Moskovskoe Shosse, and by the same Moskovskii Gates. The commandant gave his permission, and we dragged our belongings and those of others over to this two-story, wooden, incompletely constructed building. The side of the building looked out on an empty field, pitted with shell-holes.

Next to the building, we planned to create a vegetable garden in the spring, and my husband even set up something like a greenhouse for early vegetables. There were plenty of broken window-frames round about, and although these lacked glass, it was possible to collect as many glass fragments as we wanted. For the garden, my husband had stored up a little bag full of beans, a pound or a little more. Ol'ga Ivanovna knew of this bag, and perhaps for lack of a topic for conversation with the commandant, informed him that our family was taking its leave of her, and that we had a sack (!) of beans.

The result of this irresponsible babbling was that the commandant sent a *Feldwebel*[114] to us to carry out a "requisition of stocks." We succeeded in making him laugh when Sister Bednova, herself much given to joking, solemnly pulled out of a cupboard the miserable little bag full of beans. The visit, however, was not without consequences, since while looking around the apartment, he discovered three chickens. When the *Volksdeutsche*[115] were evacuated, our good friend Aleksandr Kremer[116] left them to us for 500 rubles, and we kept them there throughout the entire winter, keeping them secret from Ol'ga Ivanovna. Later, the commandant himself came for two of them, declaring that he was confiscating them for the benefit of the German army, but that he would leave one for us, since we were excellent citizens. The news of live chickens in a dead city quickly took wing, and within three days our chicken was turned into soup for Herr Edenhardt.

There was one more unpleasantness connected with the visit by the commandant. He discovered a table designed especially for coins, and proceeded to

---

[114] An NCO rank in the German army.

[115] *Volksdeutsche*—people of German ancestry.

[116] Aleksandr Veniaminovich Kremer lived on Moskovskoe Shosse. He was very likely related to the artist Veniamin Veniaminovich Kremer (1899–1977), who lived in Pushkin and who remained on Soviet territory. TsGA SPB. F. 8557. Op. 6. D. 1020. L. 292. Akty-spiski naseleniia g. Pushkin, 1944 g.; Central Archive of the Ministry of Defense of the Russian Federation (TsAMO RF). Fond Leningradskogo Voenno-peresyl'nogo punkta. Op. 530167. D. 42970. Kartochka No. 815, Kremer Veniamin Veniaminovich.

pester us, saying that he had a great love of old coins, and that we should give him the table. The table, like the apartment itself, was not ours, and we told him this, but he did not believe us. Then Ol'ga Ivanovna spoke up and assured him with great conviction that although Gospodin Bogachev was interested in many things, he had never been a numismatist. As a consolation, she pointed out to the *Feldwebel* a beautiful man's dressing gown hanging in a wardrobe of the former owner of the premises. The Germans grabbed it and took it with them.

Now without us, Ol'ga Ivanovna committed an undoubted crime. Living in her apartment was the militia member Sh., and with her permission, he set off on an expedition to obtain food. He had obtained firewood for her by demolishing fences and houses; now, she remained in the apartment without a man to perform manual tasks. The girls and their German beaus sawed firewood, but a great deal of this was needed, since everyone loved warmth. To replace the absent Sh., the city administration designated Leont'ev, who was also a militia member, but of a somewhat higher rank. Of course, Leont'ev was not especially anxious to work for the hated interpreter, and he neglected his tasks, without caring about the consequences. Ol'ga Ivanovna complained to the commandant, adding that instead of sawing wood, Leont'ev found it more agreeable to sit at home with his wife in their comfortable apartment (at that time residents found it very easy to ensure the comfort of their apartments, because furnishings could be added to from half-destroyed dwellings, or could simply be found left on the street, since people who were being evacuated could not take such things with them).

Ol'ga Ivanovna and the commandant then paid the Leont'evs a visit. The visit included a search, during which it seemed that nothing of interest to the commandant was discovered apart from some silver tablespoons, marked as dating from a very distant year. Ol'ga Ivanovna declared that Leont'ev was young, and that consequently . . . the spoons could not be his. The spoons were duly confiscated, and in passing, she took with her two pairs of shoes of her size, which she immediately put on, since at that time footwear was in very short supply even for her.

The next day, the commandant's assistant escorted Leont'ev ahead of him in the direction of the 3rd School, in the courtyard of which was a large shell hole. Standing Leont'ev on the edge of the shell-hole, the assistant shot him. Ol'ga Ivanovna struck up a friendship with Leont'ev's wife, no doubt in gratitude for the shoes and in hopes of other benefits.

Ol'ga Ivanovna remained continuously in the post of chief interpreter in the city of Pushkin, strictly observing the interests of the Germans, and only sometimes the interests of the population, when these coincided with her own interests. It is necessary to be just, and to note that she herself was interested only in food, while valuables went to her superiors. She and her daughters were so ravenous that their old nanny would always tell us, "They just stuff themselves, stuff themselves, God save us." The nanny herself ate little, started becoming bloated, and died in the hospital. I asked Ol'ga Ivanovna not to send her away, saying I would treat her and feed her myself—but Ol'ga Ivanovna did not agree.

One of Ol'ga Ivanovna's daughters, the older one, Zhenia, was wounded in the chest by a shell splinter while walking about the city with the commandant. The German doctors treated her and said that her lungs had not been affected. Ol'ga Ivanovna brought me her X-ray photos, and I found that both her pleura and lungs had been damaged. She stayed in the hospital only for a relatively short time, and then began walking about the city once again. When the German front was tottering, the whole family was hurriedly evacuated to Litzmannstadt.[117] When I was in Germany, I did not seek them out and did not see them. Not long before I departed for Australia, I was told that Zhenia had died from tuberculosis of the lungs. I had a lot of unpleasant conversations with Ol'ga Ivanovna on political topics, and there were indications that she passed this information on.

To Ol'ga Ivanovna, as to the Germans, we were *Untermenschen*.[118] She expressed surprise at our aim of somehow constructing our own Russian state after the victory of the Germans. "What structure are you talking about? The Germans will structure you however it suits the Führer."

For more than a year, while we lived in the same apartment with her or close by, she never once helped us with the food supplies she had. It is true that she had no reserves, except for two or three barrels of pickled cabbage that appeared in the apartment after a number of families had been evacuated. Quite probably, she herself had insisted on this forced evacuation, since she knew these stores existed.

There were a number of analogous cases. My family ate the cabbage too, since it was our practice to make soup in common. A large pot of boiling water stood on the continually hot stove, and we put into the pot everything we had obtained that day. For us this was the only food we had, something that could not be said of the interpreter and her daughters. They "stuffed themselves," as their domestic helper Fruzia put it, the whole day and even at night.

---

[117] Contemporary German name of occupied Łódź.
[118] Subhumans (*German*).

Just once we had a shared feast. That was when we saw in the New Year, at the beginning of 1942. There were ten Germans present. I remember that one of them brought two pounds of rice for this feast, and instructed us in long and boring detail how it needed to be cooked. Clearly, he imagined that we had never in our lives seen this luxury. Fruzia and I cooked it in line with our hungry reasoning, that is, without washing away the starch. Of course, it finished up like porridge, but very tasty, since tipped into it were milk obtained from Fekla Grigor'evna, a little German margarine, dried cherries and apples, and most important, real sugar. Everyone was satisfied, including the man who had donated the rice. The highlight of the meal was a huge piece of horsemeat, thoroughly roasted and braised with vegetables, and also pies made from the same horsemeat and black flour, beautifully prepared by the skilled hand of Iakovlev, who was a cook by profession. He was suffering cruelly from hunger, and was glad to accept our invitation to dinner. Much later he went to work as a cook for the Spaniards, and did well for himself.

I remember that we doctors were invited to lunch by the Spanish doctors on their national day, apparently November 8. To mark this day, Franco had sent each soldier a parcel, four kilograms in weight, that included various tasty items. Iakovlev set to work preparing this lunch for us, and along with everything else a huge biscuit sponge cake, with cream made from butter, stood on the table. It was adorned on top with an artistically designed swastika (of the Spanish variety, not the German), made of cream. Of course, there was also alcohol, mainly liqueurs (not only for us ladies, since the Spaniards liked them too—for example, there was a wonderful liqueur that was not exactly cumin, and something like anisc).

To top it all off, someone summoned from the unit a hairdresser with . . . a violin. He gave expert performances of a number of pieces, and in conclusion played the "Song of the Indian Guest" from the Opera "Sadko" by Rimsky-Korsakoff. While playing it, he looked intently at the four of us. Did we know the composer? To his pleasure and satisfaction, we did.

Securing nutrition: More on food

Like it or not, there is no avoiding talk of food, the very pivot of our existence at that time. Even before the Spanish division arrived, Fekla Griogor'evna's cow had been slaughtered. The meat that Sister Bednova brought over to my apartment outside the Moskovskii Gates played a decisive role in our lives. Once again, we began making soups in common with Ol'ga Ivanovna, despite not living in her apartment, since we could not avoid telling her about the meat. She was all-knowing, and if we had not told her, the meat would of course have been taken to meet the needs of the German army, just like our chickens.

This meat was directly responsible for resurrecting my husband and me. Little more remained of us by this time than our shadows. Further, my husband's arms were covered in some kind of rash, and itched unbearably. I suffered from furunculosis and lymphadenitis. At night, when everyone else was asleep, I performed operations on myself, opening the pustules. I was reluctant to abandon my husband and have myself admitted to the hospital, doing so only when it was necessary to be operated on under full anesthesia, and to have a blood transfusion.

Within a month we were unrecognizable, and people were looking at us suspiciously. That is what it means for someone to have 100 grams each day of beautiful fresh meat (it was winter, and salting the meat was unnecessary).

How I lamented then that the cow had not been slaughtered earlier! If that had been the case, Beliaev would have had a very good chance of surviving. As it was, he benefited only from a few drops of milk, something I blame myself for to this day. I was so sure that he would receive enough help from his wife—I was so hypnotized by the soup I had seen in their apartment, made of peas and the whole bucket of frozen potatoes, that the thought of an imminent *dénouement* did not enter my head. During my last visit with the milk, Beliaev's eloquent glance directed at the open door that led into the kitchen revealed his tragedy to me, but by then it was too late. It appears that Sister Bednova brought him milk on only two or three days—and then he died.

It angers me to remember that there was food both for Svetlana and for him; both mother and grandmother ate in the German kitchen (the old woman also worked for the Germans, since she spoke German). Nevertheless, I once saw them both, and also Svetlana, eating soup that had been brought home, while Aleksandr Romanovich lay nearby in an unheated room. His bed was some distance from the wall, and next to the bed was a large, tall bookshelf-cupboard. Even at that time I thought this was very dangerous, since if a shell exploded the bookshelf would fall directly onto him. I did not tell him this, since even without this there were plenty of accidents that could happen.

I remember that he was lying on the bed, dressed in a winter overcoat, and that on his head was a tall, black caracul cap. And if anything, heat was aplenty and easy to provide him with if his family had wanted. When his wife, daughter, and mother-in-law were evacuated with the *Volksdeutsche* in February 1942,

I was present as they climbed into a car next to the premises of the S.D.,[119] and I expressed my regret that Aleksandr Romanovich was not with them. I added my own thoughts on this account, but I felt sorry for her [the wife], since she was very embarrassed.

It was easy for me to talk and to judge: "Who is more dear to you, your husband or your child?" Never in my life have I had to face that question. But Ivanov-Razumnik[120] survived, and why? Probably because he and his wife had a strong bond, and if he had died, his wife would undoubtedly have followed soon after. I remember that he once called on my husband to ask about preserving his library. He looked to be in poor shape. I recall that we gave him sugar, cutting a bit off our own piece. We cut it with my surgical pincers, for lack of sugar pincers, and a piece of steel broke off them. Somehow, I have kept those pincers throughout all our subsequent wanderings, but Ivanov-Razumnik is no longer alive.[121]* Thank God, he did not die in the degrading circumstances of imprisonment and hunger.

I am glad we were able to share with him that sugar, whose origins were as follows. In Pushkin, on September 14, the shops of the Gostinyi Dvor, where all our markets and trading were concentrated, suffered a natural disaster. By that time the shops were no longer functioning. It was amusing to watch from the windows of the polyclinic as happy or fearful people dragged sacks full of something or other along the ground, or carried them on their shoulders. We did not understand immediately what was going on, but once we had worked it out, I and many others among the staff began to get angry and indignant. My surgical sister E. A. Fokina became especially furious when through the window she saw a man, a *biulletenshchik*[122] who for many years had appeared regularly at the clinic claiming to suffer from various ailments, go past laden with a huge sack. Usually, and without the burden, he had barely crawled to us to get his latest note permitting him to be off work. Possessing a very decisive, somewhat coarse na-

---

[119] *Sicherheitsdienst*—National Socialist Security Service, German intelligence agency.

[120] Razumnik Vasil'evich Ivanov (Ivanov-Razumnik) (1878–1946) was a literary scholar, sociologist, and author of a set of memoirs. After being subject to repression, he was allowed to settle in Pushkin before the war. He was evacuated to Germany thanks to the German ancestry of his wife. He kept a notebook in 1942. Ivanov died in Munich in 1946.

[121] * Note by Baskakova: *My son and I used to cut our nails with the pincers. To this day they serve for manicures.*

[122] Soviet jargon, from the word *biulleten*—in this case, a list of people unfit for work because of illness, a sick list. A *biulletenshchik* was someone constantly off work on the pretext of illness (*po biulleteniu*). In the conditions of the Soviet economy, where workers by 1940 were threatened with jail sentences if they absented themselves from work or changed their workplace independently, without the permission of their superiors, such behavior had become a whole strategy of survival.

ture, Fokina rushed out onto the street, flung herself on the "scoundrel," gave him a beating and triumphantly hauled the sack of rice, weighing three *puds*, into the dressing station. After this many other staff members of the polyclinic followed her example. They were not perhaps motivated by noble feelings of indignation at the "looters," such as had inspired Fokina, but the result was the same: here and there in the polyclinic sacks, boxes and bundles appeared. This did not last long, since the public learned of it and began thronging our street.

The things that were brought in at that time! There was tobacco, and expensive cigarettes, and granulated sugar mixed with tobacco. There was every kind of haberdashery—threads, buttons—all of it in whole boxes. For some reason there were many bags full of children's toys, as usual of very poor quality and broken as well. Toward evening the passions and excitement subsided, and a sorting-out (though not a comradely division) of the trophies began. Many were bitter at the results, since there was almost nothing of real consequence, that is, food and items of clothing. The young sisters acquired eau de cologne and other perfumes, and shamelessly powdered themselves with the best brands of cosmetics. We, that is, the workers of the surgical section, finished up with our sack of rice.

It soon became clear that the population had acted correctly. Almost all the party members made themselves scarce. The organs of the Ministry of Internal Affairs, as represented by the militia members, transformed themselves into ordinary citizens, and alongside the others, dragged off everything they could lay their hands on, while furiously dousing a fire if it blazed up somewhere, either accidentally amid the general chaos or due to the "conscientiousness" of a few Soviet citizens who recalled the instruction: "We shall not surrender anything to the enemy, we'll burn it ourselves!"[123]

In any case, the bakery burnt down. Large stores of flour perished in the flames. Under the Germans, excavations at the site continued for a lengthy period, since the flour, though smelling of smoke, had to be used. Some of this flour was seized from a resident, and he and his 14-year-old son were hanged from a pole bearing a street sign at the intersection of Ulitsa Moskovskaia and

---

[123] A Sovnarkom directive issued on June 29, 1941, to party and Soviet organizations in the front-line provinces ordered the destruction of all objects of value that could not be evacuated. In practice, this led to real chaos. On July 7, 1941, the staff of the North-Western Sector sent a telegram ordering "a halt to the arbitrary burning of the city of Pskov. Important objects will be burnt by units on their departure." On the day when Petergof was abandoned, the Bol'shoi Ekaterininskii palace was burnt; according to the Germans, it was set on fire by retreating Red Army units. There are recollections, not entirely reliable, that in Pushkin stores of foodstuffs were burnt by Young Pioneer inmates of a children's home under the direction of a girl Komsomol organizer. TsAMO. F. 221. Op. 1351. D. 168. L. 52. Telegramma gen.-maiora Rakutina ot 07.07.1941; Tsypin, *Gorod Pushkin v gody voiny*, 244–45.

Ulitsa Pervogo Maia, opposite the windows of the commandant's office, which was located in a pharmacy building.[124] On the eve of the execution, my husband saw the arrestees in the premises of the commandant's office. The boy was seated, holding in his hands a cooking-pot full of acorns that he had collected. He had evidently meant to bake flatbread cakes using the acorns and the flour.

These were the first victims of the Germans who were protecting the population against "raids by looters." Soon after, there was a woman hanging there. She had been brought into the commandant's office from the "forbidden zone," that is, from streets that at some unknown point had been declared to be such. She had been carrying a basket in which there were crystal drinking-glasses. I also remember a woman in a fur coat with a kangaroo-skin collar, wearing felt boots and with long shaggy hair, who for a prolonged period swung from a branch of an old birch tree next to the Soviet cooperative that had earlier been Gusterin's[125] colonial store. The felt boots soon disappeared; logically enough, the German soldiers took them, since they themselves suffered acutely from the cold, and were also prone to taking felt boots from living civilians who were walking in them along the street. My husband, guarding this treasure and not anxious to lose his feet to frostbite in the minus-40-degree temperatures, always wore his trousers outside his boots, and not tucked into them. That way the soldiers did not notice his beautiful felt boots covered with leather, which he had kept from his hunting days.

The woman who was hanged was guilty of cutting pieces of meat from the corpses of neighbors who had died of hunger and cold. After cooking the meat, she had eaten it herself and used it to feed two small children.[126] Many peo-

---

[124] This case is mentioned in all the testimonies by witnesses before the ChGK. Among the first to be hanged were the park forester Egor Iaritsa and his adolescent son, who had entered a forbidden zone while looking for a cow. Ivanova, *Za blokadnym kol'tsom*, 561.

[125] The Fedor Gusterin store on the corner of Ulitsa Oranzhereinaia (Ulitsa Kominterna) and Ulitsa Malaia (Ulitsa Revoliutsii).

[126] Other witnesses to the occupation remembered similar things. Baskakova, though, names the next intersection, Ulitsa Revoliutsii and Ulitsa Kominterna, and not Ulitsa Revoliutsii and Ulitsa Pervogo Maia. Witnesses testified: "A woman was hanged on Ulitsa Pervogo Maia next to building No. 10 in the winter of 1942," and "on the corner of Ulitsa Revoliutsii and Ulitsa Pervogo Maia a woman was hanged with a sign on her chest saying 'For eating her child.'" It is known that in neighboring Pavlovsk on April 7, 1942, Natal'ia Andreeva was executed in the city market. Andreeva had revealed that she had first dug up corpses in the cemetery, and had then resorted to murdering people and to feeding her children with the meat she obtained. Despite the shocking nature of such accounts, cases of this kind remained within the bounds of statistical error, even as innumerable rumors grew up around them. TsGA SPB. F. 8557. Op. 6. D. 1095. L. 69, 76. Zaiavlenie A. (identified only by her initial in the document) Aleksandrovoi v chrezvychainuiu komissiiu po rassledovaniiu zlodeianii, February 28, 1944; Ob'iasneniia Aleksandry Konstantinovny Melkumovoi, February 1944; TsGA SPB. F. 9788b. Op. 1. D. 31. L. 41–47. Sicherheitspolizei u. S.D., Aussenstelle Pawlowsk, Vernehmungsniederschrift der Andreewna Natalia. April 3, 1942. On cannibalism in Pushkin and Pavlovsk during the winter of 1941–1942, see Rutherford, *Combat and Genocide*, 152.

ple were indignant at this injustice. For some reason, it was permissible to eat half-rotten cats, dogs, and horses dug from beneath the snow in spring (the horses had been killed by shellfire and had not been butchered, since people at first were not starving; instead, the dead horses had been fed upon by dogs). I knew a woman, a medical orderly in Pavlovsk, who traded in cuts of such meat.

Sister Bednova, to whom people used to turn for advice, related that the entire store of potassium permanganate had been used for the purpose of soaking horse meat. And indeed, it was better that the canteen and workers of the polyclinic were supplied with horse meat, since the horses were already dead. I personally saw a horse suspended from the ceiling in the stables; a driver told me that there had been a three-day wait for a load of hay to arrive, and that the horse did not live to see it delivered.

Among the people who were hanged was our acquaintance, the engineer Kapustin. Under the Germans, he began working in the mechanical plant, where he had also been employed earlier. He had a great fear of hunger, and somehow managed to secure a transfer to Gatchina, where he had been promised a ration and an apartment. After spending a certain time there, he decided that the promises to him were not being fulfilled. Incautiously and light-mindedly, he then returned to Pushkin. His former co-worker at the plant, the medical assistant Bednova, met him on the street and set about trying to persuade him somehow to return, and in the meantime, at least to hide himself in her apartment. With incomprehensible stubbornness, Kapustin declared his displeasure with the Germans who, he declared, had deceived him, and nevertheless went first to the plant, and then to the commandant. Two days later he was hanged at the same intersection, for willfully quitting his job.[127]

I remember a few other cases, but these victims will suffice. I would, though, like to mention my colleague, the ophthalmologist Dr. Kantsel'. He was Jewish, but I think had been christened, since he had remained in Pushkin. The population of the city disliked him for his rudeness in dealing with them, and his workmates for his arrogance and condescension. During the first days of the occupation, when the hunt for Jews had not yet begun, Dr. Kantsel' was hanged in the Aleksandrovskii Park.[128]

---

[127] Kapustin's execution is mentioned by several witnesses to the occupation, including Ivanov-Razumnik. Witness Mansurov recalled that the engineer (whom he named Sorokin, not Kapustin) left the Pushkin plant because of an argument with Sokovnin. Amherst College/The Ivanov-Razumnik diary. Entry from January 2, 1942; TsGA SPB. F. 8557. Op. 6. D. 1095. L. 32. Protokol doprosa Petra Matveevicha Mansurova, February 19, 1944.

[128] This is the sole mention in the text of the extermination of the Pushkin Jews.

Throwback: 1941

The declaration of war on June 22, 1941, was met by the Soviet people with joyful excitement, artfully concealed behind a mask of anxious preoccupation and a decent degree of hustle and bustle.

In the House of Culture, a medical commission was set up to examine those going to the front. We were immediately given a list of the medical conditions that were no longer to be taken into account, and almost everyone who under the old provisions would have been declared unsuitable was now considered fit for service. The large premises were completely occupied by mobilized men with their knapsacks and bundles, and the mood was one of excitement. Coming from the stage were speeches by agitators and our medical lectures (blood transfusions were my topic).[129] We three doctors took turns being on duty there at night. We were in excellent spirits, but not in the least because we were eager to fight "for the homeland, for Stalin," but because the fighting at the front and the general chaos round about meant that the collapse of the authorities was approaching. The Germans were already in Luga, and at that time it did not occur to us to wonder whether life with them would be better for us or worse.[130] It was clear to everyone that for things to be worse was impossible.

While working in the commission we became acquainted with the commission staff, and received access to all the benefits available to military personnel in our country. We ate in the Leninskii village, where we enjoyed cutlets at a fabulously cheap price. On each floor of the House of Culture itself, buffets had been set up that were richly supplied with food of all kinds. Since these also served the whole mass of mobilized soldiers, there were no delicacies, but there were sausages of various kinds, lard, bread, bread rusks, and bagels. Like many of the other people there I was very attracted to the bagels, which quickly disappeared. It was then necessary to appeal to acquaintances among the buffet workers, on the basis of favoritism. Every day I took several pounds home, and in this way built up a reserve that became extremely useful when we were sitting in the bomb shelter.

---

[129] A political report from June 27, 1941, states: "Doctors of the medical center held two discussions on blood transfusions." The topics of the political discussions conducted by agitators during the first days of the war were relatively diverse, ranging from reading the brochure "A warrior of the RKKA does not submit to capture" to personal hygiene. Central State Archive of Historical-Political Documents of Saint-Petersburg (TsGAIPD SPB). F. 2242. Op. 1. D. 515. L. 14, 139. Politdonesenie voennogo otdela Pushkinskogo raikoma VPK(b) ot 26 i 27 iiunia 1941.

[130] The Germans occupied Luga on August 24, 1941.

The work itself was difficult, unpleasant, and outright dangerous, especially for a surgeon who in addition was not a party member. If a mobilized man was entitled for some reason to exemption from service, a formal interrogation began, involving threats and so on from the party section of the recruiting commission. Before long I left, since in the polyclinic there was a great deal of work in the traumatological department, in addition to which "barracks conditions" had been declared. We were now having to treat war wounds, both among the civilian population and also among troops from the front, which as the soldiers told us was at Iam-Izhora.[131] I remember that a young lieutenant was delivered to us with his arm almost torn off. An inpatient department with cots was also set up in the polyclinic. Undressing the lieutenant involved taking off his beautiful boots, over which two orderlies almost came to blows after the owner of the boots had died.

Everyone moved down to the cellar, which had been transformed in timely fashion into a reasonably good bomb shelter.[132] There was work for both day and night. The wounded who were lying in bed remained up above; indeed, there was not even enough room for those who were sitting. The civilian population were crammed in with us as well, as we lacked the strength to refuse them. The bombardment continued almost without letup, and the entire building rocked. Next, we saw huge shell holes opposite the entrance. One night we heard a truck draw up. Someone ran into the corridor where we were all seated, and began calling for a certain "Valia" to go with him, since the Germans were close and there was not a minute to lose. This "Valia" turned out to be a sister from the tuberculosis dispensary, and the officer was her brother. She refused outright to go with him. "I'm more scared of you than of the Germans!" she shouted in the darkness.

Sitting up above were soldiers, for the most part.[133]

---

[131] Iam-Izhora—a settlement on the Moskovskoe Shosse, on the banks of the River Izhora. On August 29, Iam-Izhora was captured by the 122nd Infantry Division. Soviet forces managed to hold positions on the northern bank of the river and tried repeatedly to reclaim the settlement.

[132] In Leningrad and its suburbs, bomb and gas shelters were prepared as early as the beginning of 1941. In March, the city commission found that the number of them in Pushkin was categorically inadequate: only in school No. 5 and in the city hospital on Sovetskii Bul'var had the cellars been adapted in order to provide shelter. TsGAIPD SPB. F. 2242. Op. 1. D. 515. L. 21–26. Materialy po voennoi rabote Pushkinskogo raikoma BKP(b), 1–31 marta 1941 g.

[133] Break in the text. The fall of Pushkin on September 17 was one of the most obscure and mythologized episodes of the beginning of the Leningrad blockade, an episode that has become overgrown with a multitude of urban myths and legends. These center on the claim that the regular forces and party chiefs deliberately abandoned the suburb, something that is not confirmed by operational documents. Soviet forces encircled near Luga broke through and were chaotically retreating through Pushkin, at the same time as the local command tried to launch a counterattack against the enemy with the help of hastily assembled combat groups. Baskakova's recollec-

On September 17, someone arrived and said he had seen a German on horseback on Ulitsa Pervogo Maia. How credible this was I cannot say, but it ran through us like an electric current, and many people, including myself and my son, began hurriedly preparing to go "home." There was a feeling that the end of the war was at hand, and indeed, there was less shooting that day. We took some of our suitcases, and from the darkness that had enveloped us for many days, went out into God's clear light. Without any pangs of conscience, I left my wounded to the care of Sister Fokina, who declared that she had nowhere to go, since her house was already burnt.

I remember how we passed by the devastated Gostinyi Dvor, to which my son ran, but with no results. One thing and another remained there, but nothing that was to his taste. Nevertheless, people were pulling things out and carrying them off. Before us walked an old woman, carrying beneath her arm a quite large mirror, while in her other hand was a sack, from a hole in which poured a stream of lentils. At the very end of Ulitsa Moskovskaia a shell burst; we flung ourselves down and lay prone. When we stood up, the old woman was nowhere to be seen. We did not go home to Moskovskoe Shosse, but turned aside into the bomb shelter of the 1st School, there to spend an entire month. In our section of the shelter there were many teachers. Everyone lay on the floor and on their bundles, and next to us was Ol'ga Ivanovna Videman.

The people in the shelter had known nothing of the arrival of the Germans, and were delighted at the news we brought. They showed their pleasure by pulling out their food stores, and set about treating us to beautiful "Krasnaia Moskva" sweets, bringing out an entire box. But this was only for the purposes of celebration, and once days of hunger set in, it was no more. Everyone sat on their food reserves and ate unnoticed, rustling their possessions quietly as they drew one thing or another from the depths of their bundles. The rumors about the Germans were confirmed the next day, and with each day thereafter further news was reported. Either it was that the Germans had visited the hospital and the pharmacy, obtaining alcohol, morphine, and cocaine, or else an elder from the Znamenie Church had come running in to relate that he had seen a German officer kneeling and praying before an icon of the Mother of God, or we were informed that they were grabbing men on the street, especially young men, putting them behind bars and then carting them off to be put to work.

---

tions, despite contributing nothing to the history of the military operations, are typical in that they show precisely the chaos and the absence of information available to ordinary people, the two factors they were cognizant of at the time.

All this was later confirmed. Sister Fokina sent me my share of the rice, which suited us very well. On a few occasions we left the shelter and went home. Despite the bombardment we were not frightened, and it seemed as though the war was about to end. Arriving home, I first of all poisoned our wonderful sheepdog. For this purpose, I had long since prepared strychnine. It was said that the Germans were shooting dogs and cats. The second thing we did was to bring back inside the things we had earlier taken out into the garden, and to restore them to their usual places. It appeared that soon everything would come to an end, and that we would begin living a free, peaceful life.

So that the "liberators" would not casually make off with things we needed, we dug a hole in the chicken coop and placed in it our dishes and valuable old porcelain. We also buried a certain amount of food in a small metal trunk. Our vegetable patch and the garden had been torn up by shells. Our neighbor Ol'ga Ivanovna Videman left the cellar entirely and moved back into her apartment, saying this was now safe. What might be called a staff immediately gathered around her, and her fortunes rose. Coming home once to the apartment, we found there a whole company of Germans—not without the kind help of Ol'ga Ivanovna, I think, a medical unit had been stationed there with us.

A number of doctors sat in armchairs, leafing through our albums and reading my medical books and journals. They greeted us without special politeness, although I had been recommended to them as a doctor and as a householder. Embarrassed, we turned and without taking anything, departed. I noted that the covers had been taken from the furniture, and all the vases had been filled with fresh flowers, primarily dahlias, of which we had many varieties. The stove had been lit, and the soldiers were frying our potatoes in lard.

The bombardment of the city continued, but the shells were now Russian. Everywhere fires were breaking out, and it was frightening at night to observe this sea of flame and to hear the dull sound as buildings collapsed. We went out onto the broad courtyard of the school and tried to guess what was burning, while the especially enterprising even ran out onto the street and headed for the place that was on fire. Through this method, a certain number of members of the public acquired stores of flour when a nearby bakery burnt down.

It was this fire, with its numerous casualties, that forced me to organize an infirmary in our part of the cellar. One room was cleared out. Beds were gathered from various sources, to be covered with boards and rags. The frightening picture of this infirmary will never vanish from my memory. The complete darkness and limited amount of water multiplied the difficulties of my work. A little oil-lamp was my salvation. The injuries that needed treatment were extremely diverse, from small scratches to cavity wounds of the abdomen and chest. At that time the hospital did not exist, and in any case, transporting the injured there would have been physically impossible. Overloaded with work, I tried in vain to secure the help of my surgical sister Fokina from the polyclinic—she herself had a great deal of work there.

Sister B.,[134] who was also in the bomb shelter, came to my aid. Her tireless energy made its effects felt in everything. She went out under gunfire to fetch water, and risking the bullets she made her way onto the territory of the nearby hospital, from which she obtained dressing materials and even medications. There was a complete lack of serums, and to this day it remains a mystery to me why we did not see severe infections such as gas cellulitis and tetanus. The number of deaths was small. A month of working under such conditions saw me lose more than a *pud* of fat, but strengthened me spiritually to the extent that I managed to endure the whole two years of the German occupation without losing my human dignity.

It was only in November that the cellar was emptied. My family moved in with the interpreter, and the remaining patients who were seriously injured but could be expected to recover were transferred first to tolerable accommodation, and then to a newly organized civilian hospital in Sofiia.

By this time the city of Pushkin had revived, since everyone had crawled out of their burrows, and passers-by now appeared on the streets. It was in vain, however, that people dreamed of the beginning of an era of freedom, while trying to adapt to the new living conditions. The Germans, who at first had seemed like noble conquerors, were not slow to reveal their actual, "Aryan" character. All kinds of figurative scorpions promptly rained down on us. More than half of the city was declared by the commandant to be a "forbidden zone," and people who had just returned to their apartments were required not even within 24 hours but in a lesser time to move to unknown locations. Once again there was a stream of victims of German bullets, people who could not manage and perhaps did not wish to obey the order. Of course, this was war in all its cruelty and . . . sentimentality. From when I was in the polyclinic, I recall how a German soldier brought to me, in his arms, an adolescent girl whom he had wounded in the leg. She had been going to her home on Moskovskoe Shosse, which was now a forbidden zone.

---

[134] Evidently, Bednova.

Then came the rounding up of young men and youths.[135] Their mothers ran in tears to the commandant, but everything was in vain, and many of them lost their sons forever. Two of my son's comrades came back to us after four months, but in what a state, and with what an appearance! One was Igor' Chichagov, the son of a music teacher; he was as thin as a skeleton and covered in lice. The boys had been held behind barbed wire near Gatchina, in the open (this was in minus-thirty-degree temperatures), and had not been put to work. Igor' then tracked down his mother and sisters, who were working for the Germans. He was a very talented musician and composer who had been studying at the Leningrad Conservatory, receiving a stipend of 500 rubles per month. He is now married to my son's former classmate Kira Baklanova, who has a beautiful soprano voice. After living in Germany, where both of them gave concerts, they settled in America. Success has followed them there as well.[136]

Following the roundups came a mass evacuation of residents from Pushkin, since the city had ended up being located in a strip next to the front line. The residents, who firmly believed that any day soon St. Petersburg would be captured and that the end was approaching for the Bolsheviks, desperately resisted being shipped out. Not even the hunger that had already taken off hundreds of people restrained them. Many rushed to the doctors in the polyclinic to obtain certificates attesting to illnesses that would prevent them temporarily from being evacuated. Initially this worked, and the evacuations were either cancelled altogether, or else only insignificant numbers of people were sent, individuals who thought it prudent to go or who simply wanted to. I remember one evacuation in which people were herded onto trucks using rubber truncheons. Evacuation took place on a mass scale in February 1942, when it involved the

---

[135] On September 28, 1941, the commander of the 18th Army, Colonel-General Georg von Küchler, ordered the deportation of all men aged between 15 and 55 years from the front line zone. The deportees were held as "civilian prisoners" (*Zivilgefangene*) in transit camps (*Durchgangslager—Dulag*) in Gatchina and Rozhdestveno. In some cases, civilians were accommodated in prisoner-of-war camps. In all these places the conditions of detention were inhuman. People were not fed and were unable to shelter themselves from the cold (often, they lived in holes dug in the ground) or to wash. By November 30, some 4,183 people were being held in the "civilian camps" of the 18th Army. In December, most of the survivors began to be released and to be allowed to return to their relatives. TsGA SPB. F. 9788. Op. 1. D. 69. L. 31. Einsatzgruppe A Stab, "Befehl," November 30, 1941; Hürter, "Die Wehrmacht vor Leningrad," 411.

[136] Igor' Evgen'evich Chichagov graduated with distinction in 1941 from the school of the Leningrad Conservatory. He was married to Kira Baklanova. In November 1949, the couple left Germany for the USA. From 1954, Igor' Chichagov was Director of the Baltimore Opera. Kira died in 2014, and Igor' in 2018. "Iunye muzykanty," *Muzykal'nye Kadry*, no. 22, November 14, 1940, 3; Online Archive of the Bad Arolsen Archives, Registration and Files of Displaced Persons, Children and Missing Persons, Evidence of Abode and Emigration—Emigrations, Reference Code 81712260; E. A. Aleksandrov, *Russkie v Severnoi Amerike: biograficheskii slovar'*, ed. K. M. Aleksandrov and A. V. Tereshchuk (Hamden, San Francisco, Saint-Petersburg: Filologicheskii fakul'tet SPbGU, 2005), 560.

so-called *Volksdeutsche*. Later came the evacuation of young people, sometimes along with their parents, to work in Germany. At that time my family too
sought to leave, but without result, since we were all "needed by the Germans."

I have already related a great deal from this period of the occupation, and there
is much more that could be told, but it is better not to return to those horrors.

Exit Pushkin: The last year beyond the siege

After a year of the German occupation, no more than a thousand residents remained in the city. One further evacuation had occurred; the knitwear factory
and its equipment, down to the last screw, had been carted off to Germany, and
its mostly female workers had been evacuated to Gatchina. In this case too, the
evacuation did not pass off without gunfire and rubber truncheons. The house
of Aleksei Tolstoi,[137] which at that time accommodated women workers, and
where my family lived as well, was cleared out, and the remaining people were
housed in the vast dormitory of the agricultural institute, where they were locked
up tightly for six months. In March 1942[138] we were all sent to Gatchina and its
environs, where the Germans again organized mechanical and repair workshops of all kinds. One of them was headed by my husband, while I remained
unemployed, since the hospital in Gatchina had a sufficient number of doctors.

After Pushkin, life there seemed to us the height of peace, tranquility, and
where food was concerned, abundance. True, there was still shelling and bombing, but nevertheless there were thousands of people living round about and
seemingly engaged in peaceful labor. There was a large market with a horde
of swindlers and speculators.[139] There was a good cathedral church,[140] which

---

[137] A two-story mansion on Ulitsa Proletarskaia (Tserkovnaia) was rented by the distinguished Soviet writer Aleksei Tolstoi in 1928, when he settled in Detskoe Selo. After the Soviet *maître* moved
to Moscow in 1938, the mansion was transferred to the Leningrad Writers Organization, and
a House of Creativity was organized in it.

[138] A clear slip of the pen: only 1943 makes sense.

[139] The scale of speculation and the rise of prices on the black market were so great that the occupiers took measures to restrict prices. In Pavlovsk, controls on food prices were introduced in the
summer of 1942. TsGA SPB. F. 3355. Op. 10. D. 271. L. 174. *Politseiskie Vedomosti (Pavlovsk)*, no. 7,
July 10, 1942, 3.

[140] The Cathedral of the Holy Apostle Paul in Gatchina, closed by the Soviet authorities in 1938, was
reopened after the beginning of the German occupation. The rector of the cathedral, the Arch-
priest Aleksandr Petrov, was shot by the occupiers in Gatchinskii Park in August 1942 for "anti-
German activity." His place was taken by Fedor Zabelin from the Znamenie Church in Pushkin.
TsGA SPB. F. 8557. Op. 6. D. 1095. L. 103–18. Zaiavlenie nastoiatelia Gatchinskogo Pavlovskogo
sobora protoiereia Fedora Zabelina, February 9, 1944; Raport protoiereia Fedora Zabelina lenin-
gradskomu mitropolitu Aleksiiu, February 9, 1944.

was continually being refurbished. All the best residential buildings were occupied by German units. Every scrap of land next to these buildings was painstakingly cultivated, sown with lettuce and radishes, and enclosed by a fence made of unsawn birch trunks. Birchwood gates were also erected in the form of an arch. It was all very nice, but the birch groves and avenues round about had been destroyed.

My husband and I sought to leave Gatchina as well, but nothing came of this, and we reached no further than Elizavetino station in the Volosovskii region. At this time the evacuation of the Finns,[141] compulsory of course, was under way all around us. The poor people were grief-stricken at leaving their homes of many years. A few, sensing the possible departure of the Germans, made great efforts to delay their departure. As the Finns left, they abandoned their beautifully constructed houses, which they sometimes managed to sell for gold or for warm fur clothes. We took part in this barter too, exchanging two massive engagement rings and two fur coats for a good, sturdy house, its construction not fully complete.[142] As consolation to the Finnish peasant, we promised to return all this if he were to come back, and gave him a written receipt with this undertaking.

After our arrival we lived in someone else's apartment and waited for the Finns to be evacuated, so that we could move into the house we had purchased. But this was not how it worked out! The house was occupied by a German unit that stayed there for a whole month. Finally, the unit left, and we began setting ourselves up in our new dwelling (by my count, our seventh). The house consisted of just two large rooms, and up above, three of the attic type. In past summers, the Finn had let out these rooms for people to live in while

---

[141] The registration and evacuation of the Finnish population, like the relocation of the *Volksdeutsche*, took place in waves beginning with the winter of 1941–1942. By the summer of 1942, the 18th Army had evacuated around 10,000 people. In 1943, a new registration took place on the territory of Ingermanlandiia (Ingria), and some 49,908 Finns were counted in the army rear. By 1944, a total of 63,205 people had been evacuated to Finland, including from Estonia. According to Soviet data, only a little more than 1000 Finns remained on the territory abandoned by the Germans. For the Finnic-speaking minorities of Leningrad Province, who had already suffered assimilation and Stalinist repression, the Second World War was the final blow that did away with their ethnic identity. Not even the people who managed to return home after their forced deportation could count on reestablishing their cultural-linguistic autonomy. TsGA SPB. F. 9788. Op. 1. D. 59. L. 106. Befehlshaber d.Sipo u.SD. "Ostland," 31.05.1942; BArch Freiburg, RH 23/281, Bl. 12. Korück 583 Abt. VII, Aktemvermerk zur Abstammung der um den finn. Meerbusen siedeln-den finn.-ugrischen Volksstämme, July 3, 1943; V. Musaev, *Politicheskaia istoriia Ingermanlandii v kontse XIX–XX veke* (Saint-Petersburg: Izdatel'stvo 'Nestor-Istoriia,' 2003), 303–4.

[142] A further example of the barter trade that never ceased throughout the entire occupation. In Pavlovsk in March 1942, stories circulated of people who had exchanged a *pud* of potatoes for an expensive fur that they sold at a high price near Pskov, going on to buy a house in Narva. TsGA SPB. F. 9788. Op. 1. D. 7. L. 70 Aussenstelle SD Pawlowsk. Stimmungs- und Lagebericht 11–25.03.42.

they worked on their dacha plots, but I used them to accommodate a mother hen and her chickens.

The commandant turned out to have been the head doctor of the hospital in Gatchina to which I had gone with a request to be granted permission to work as a doctor. At that time, he had very politely refused, saying that the hospital was to leave within a few days. Turns out, they had left for the same place my family moved to. When I encountered this doctor in Elizavetino I did not recognize him, but he remembered me. He did not propose that I come and work with him, but at that point I did not want to either, since I had a full load in the Russian hospital and among the population. The name of the head doctor in the Russian hospital was L-p.[143]

The local population, who were not experiencing hunger, took a very sympathetic attitude to us people from Pushkin, and many of them helped us, including[144]

---

[143] This name could not be determined.
[144] Final break in the text.

Bibliography

Archives

Australia
National Archives of Australia (NAA)

Germany
Bundesarchiv–Militärarchiv Freiburg (BArch Freiburg)
Bundesarchiv Berlin (BArch Berlin)

Russian Federation
Central Archive of the Ministry of Defense of the Russian Federation (TsAMO RF)
Central State Archive of Historical-Political Documents of Saint-Petersburg (Ts-GAIPD SPB)
Central State Archive of Saint-Petersburg (TsGA SPB)
Central State Historical Archive of Saint-Petersburg (TsGIA SPB)
Russian State Military Archive (RGVA)
State Archive of the Russian Federation (GARF)

United States of America
Amherst College, MA. Amherst Center for Russian Culture. The Archive Collection
Stanford University, Hoover Institution Archives (HIA)
The Archive of the Museum of Russian Culture, San Francisco
The National Archives and Records Administration, Washington DC (NARA)

Newspapers

Bol'shevistskoe Slovo
Commonwealth of Australia Gazette
Muzykal'nye Kadry
Novoe Russkoe Slovo
Novoe Slovo (Berlin)
Politseiskie Vedomosti (Pavlovsk)
Severnoe Slovo
Za Rodinu

Online Resources

Find a Grave. https://www.findagrave.com/.
Kniga Pamiati zhertv politicheskikh repressii Novgorodskoi oblasti. http://lists.memo.ru/.
Online Archive of the Bad Arolsen Archives. https://collections.arolsen-archives.org/.
Pamiati geroev Velikoi voiny 1914–1918. https://gwar.mil.ru/.
Petrov, Igor. https://labas.livejournal.com/tag/осипова.
Prozhito. https://prozhito.org/.

Published Primary Sources

Aleksandrov, E. A. *Russkie v Severnoi Amerike: biograficheskii slovar'.* Edited by K.
    M. Aleksandrov and A. V. Tereshchuk. Hamden, San Francisco, Saint-Peters-
    burg: Filologicheskii fakul'tet SPbGU, 2005.

Ariian, P. N. *Pervyi zhenskii kalendar' na 1900 g.* Saint-Petersburg: Tovarishchestvo
    pechati i izdatel'skogo dela "Trud," 1900.

Beliaeva, S. A. *Vospominaniia ob ottse.* Saint-Petersburg: Serebrianyi vek, 2009.

Beyda, Oleg, and Xosé M. Núñez Seixas, eds. *Ispanskaia grust': Golubaia diviziia i
    pokhod v Rossiu, 1941–1942 gg.; vospominaniia V. I. Kovalevskogo.* Moscow, Saint-
    Petersburg: Nestor-Istoriia, 2021.

Budnitskii, O. V. and G. S. Zelenina, eds. *"Svershilos'. Prishli nemtsy!": Ideinyi kol-
    laboratsionizm v SSSR v period Velikoi Otechestvennoi voiny.* Moscow: Rossiis-
    kaia politicheskaia entsiklopediia [ROSSPEN], 2012.

Drabkin, Artiom, and Bair Irincheev, eds. *"A zori zdes' gromkie": Zhenskoe litso voiny.*
    Moscow: Iauza, 2012.

Ignatiev, A. A. *Piat'desiat let v stroiu.* Vol. 1. Moscow: Voenizdat, 1986.

Irincheev, Bair, Mikhail Zinov'ev, Viacheslav Davydkin et al., eds. *Sestry po oruzhiiu:
    Vospominaniia o Velikoi Otechestvennoi voine.* Vyborg: Izdatel'stvo "Voenno-is-
    toricheskii tsentr peresheika," 2016–2017.

Ivanova, I. A., ed. *Za blokadnym kol'tsom: Sbornik vospominanii zhitelei Leningrad-
    skoi oblasti vremen germanskoi okkupatsii 1941–1944 gg.* Saint-Petersburg:
    Vesti, 2010.

Kornatovskii, N. A. *Bor'ba za krasnyi Petrograd.* Moscow: Izd-vo AST, 2004.

Lomagin, N. A. *V tiskakh goloda: Blokada Leningrada v dokumentakh germanskikh
    spetssluzhb, NKVD i pis'makh leningradtsev.* 2nd ed. Saint-Petersburg: Avrora-
    Dizain, 2014.

Nikiforova, Antonina A. *Povest' o bor'be i druzhbe.* Leningrad: Lenizdat, 1967.

Núñez Seixas, Xosé M., and Oleg Beyda, eds. *An Anti-Communist on the Eastern Front: The Memoirs of a Russian Officer in the Spanish Blue Division (1941–1942)*. Yorkshire–Philadelphia: Pen & Sword Books Ltd., 2023.

Nuridzhanova, S. A., ed. *Zhizn' v okkupatsii i pervye poslevoennye gody: Pushkin-Gatchina-Estoniia; Dnevnik Liusi Khordikainen*. Saint-Petersburg: Nestor-Istoriia, 2011.

Panova, Vera. *Moio i tol'ko moio: O moei zhizni, knigakh i chitateliakh*. Saint-Petersburg: Zhurnal "Zvezda," 2005.

Pavlovskaia, A. I., and N. A. Lomagin, eds. *"Ia znaiu, chto tak pisat' nel'zia": Fenomen blokadnogo dnevnika*. Saint-Petersburg: Izdatel'stvo Evropeiskogo universiteta v Sankt-Peterburge, 2021.

Pavlovskii, A. F., and N. A. Lomagin, eds. *"Vy, naverno, iz Leningrada?": Dnevniki evakuirovannykh iz blokadnogo goroda*. Saint-Petersburg: Izdatel'stvo Evropeiskogo universiteta v Sankt-Peterburge, 2023.

Ves' Leningrad i Leningradskaia oblast': adresnaia i spravochnaia kniga na 1930 god. Chast' 1. Ves' Leningrad. Leningrad, 1928.

Ves' Petrograd na 1917 god. Petrograd: A. S. Suvorin, 1917.

Vinogradov, Aleksei, and Albert Jan Pleysier. *Okkupatsiia Leningradskoi oblasti v gody Velikoi Otechestvennoi Voiny*. Saint-Petersburg: Izdatel'stvo "LEMA," 2006.

Vsia Moskva: Adresnaia i spravochnaia kniga na 1914 g. Moscow: Izdatel'stvo A. S. Suvorina "Novoe Vremia," 1914.

Secondary Sources

Alexopoulos, Golfo. "Portrait of a Con Artist as a Soviet Man." *Slavic Review* 57, no. 4 (1998): 774–90.

Assman, Aleida. *Dlinnaia ten' proshlogo: memorial'naia kul'tura i istoricheskaia politika*. Moscow: Novoe literaturnoe obozrenie, 2014.

Balakshina, Iuliia. *Bratsvo revnitelei tserkovnogo obnovleniia (gruppa "332-kh" peterburgskikh sviashchennikov), 1903–1907*. Moscow: Sviato-Filaretovskii Institut, 2015.

Barskova, P., and R. Nikolozi, eds. *Blokadnye narrativy*. Moscow: Novoe Literaturnoe Obozrenie, 2017.

Barskova, Polina. *Sed'maia shcheloch': Teksty i sud'by blokadnykh poetov*. Saint-Petersburg: Izdatel'stvo Ivana Limbakha, 2020.

Bogoslovskii sbornik Pravoslavnogo Sviato-Tikhonovskogo bogoslovskogo instituta, no. 3b. Moscow, 1999.

Bol'shakova, N. V. *Argunovskie mastera: V dvukh chastiakh; Chast' 1*. Moscow: Kompaniia Sputnik, 2006.

Dolinina, A. A. *Nevol'nik dolga: Nauchnaia biografiia akademika I. Iu. Krachkovskogo*. Saint-Petersburg: Tsents "Peterburgskoe Vostokovedenie," 1994.

Fitzpatrick, Sheila. *Tear Off the Masks! Identity and Imposture in 20th Century Russia*. Princeton and Oxford: Princeton University Press, 2005.

———. *White Russians, Red Peril: A Cold War History of Migration to Australia*. Melbourne: La Trobe University Press, in conjunction with Black Inc., 2021.

———. "The World of Ostap Bender: Soviet Confidence Men in the Stalin Period," *Slavic Review* 61, no. 3 (2002): 535–57.

Harris, Jonathan, ed. *Writing the Siege of Leningrad: Women's Diaries, Memoirs, and Documentary Prose*. Pittsburgh, PA: University of Pittsburgh Press, 2002.

Hass, Jeffrey K. *Wartime Suffering and Survival: The Human Condition under Siege in the Blockade of Leningrad, 1941–1944*. Oxford: Oxford University Press, 2021.

Heinzen, James. *The Art of the Bribe: Corruption under Stalin 1943–1953*. New Haven and London: Yale University Press, 2016.

Hürter, Johannes. "Die Wehrmacht vor Leningrad: Krieg und Besatzungspolitik der 18. Armee im Herbst und Winter 1941/42." *Vierteljahrshefte für Zeitgeschichte* 49, no. 3 (2001): 377–440.

Iarov, Sergei. *Blokadnaia etika: Predstavleniia o morali v Leningrade v 1941–1942 gg.* Moscow: Tsentrpoligraf, 2012.

——— [Yarov, Sergey]. *Leningrad, 1941–1942: Morality in a City under Siege*. Translated by Arch Tait. Cambridge: Polity Press, 2017.

Istoriia literatury; Poetika; Kino: Sbornik v chest' Marietty Omarovny Chudakovoi. Moscow: Novoe izdatel'stvo, 2013.

Ivanov-Razumnik: Lichnost'; Tvorchestvo; Rol' v kul'ture. Saint-Petersburg: V. Belous, 1996.

Izmozik V. S., and N. B. Lebina. *Peterburg sovetskii: "Novyi chelovek" v starom prostranstve; 1920–1930-e gody; sotsial'no–arkhitekturnoe mikroistoricheskoe issledovanie*. Saint-Petersburg: Kriga, 2016.

Judt, Tony. *Postwar: A History of Europe since 1945*. New York: The Penguin Press, 2005.

Kharkhordin, Oleg. *Oblichat' i litsemerit': genealogiia rossiiskoi lichnosti*. Saint-Petersburg: Izdatel'stvo Evropeiskogo universiteta v Sankt-Peterburge, 2016.

Kilian, Jürgen. *Wehrmacht und Besatzungsherrschaft im Russischen Nordwesten 1941–1944: Praxis und Alltag im Militärverwaltungsgebiet der Heeresgruppe Nord*. Paderborn: Ferdinand Schöningh, 2012.

Kirschenbaum, Lisa A. *The Legacy of the Siege of Leningrad, 1941–1995: Myth, Memories, and Monuments*. Cambridge: Cambridge University Press, 2006.

Kostolomov, M. *Tsvety na koliuchei vetke: Krasnyi krest zhiznennogo puti profes-sora Tsaidlera; Wiborgiana Kraevedcheskie ocherki.* Kerama: Kerammiks, 2010.

Kotkin, Stephen. *Magnetic Mountain: Stalinism as a Civilization.* Berkeley: University of California Press, 1995.

Lebina, Natalia. *Sovetskaia povsednevnost': normy i anomalii; Ot voennogo kommu-nizma k bol'shomu stiliu.* Moscow: Novoe Literaturnoe Obozrenie, 2016.

Lipovetsky, Mark. "Ostap Bender: The King is Born." In *Charms of the Cynical Reason: Tricksters in Soviet and Post-Soviet Culture*, 89–124. Boston, MA: Academic Studies Press, 2011.

Masanov, I. F. *Slovar' psevdonimov russkikh pisatelei, uchenykh i obshchestvennykh deiatelei.* Vol. 4. Moscow, 1960.

Musaev, V. *Politicheskaia istoriia Ingermanlandii v kontse XIX–XX veke.* Saint-Petersburg: Izdatel'stvo "Nestor-Istoriia," 2003.

Nuñez Seixas, Xosé M. "Good Invaders? The Occupation Policy of the Spanish Blue Division in Northwestern Russia, 1941-1944." *War in History* 25, no. 3 (2018): 361-86.

———. "Russia and the Russians in the Eyes of the Spanish Blue Division Soldiers, 1941-4." *Journal of Contemporary History* 52, no. 2 (2017): 352–74.

Nuñez Seixas, Xosé M., and Oleg Beyda. "'Defeat, Victory, Repeat': Russian Émigrés between the Spanish Civil War and Operation Barbarossa, 1936–1944." *Contemporary European History* (2023): 1–16, https://doi.org/10.1017/S0960777323000085.

Orlov, D. "Kto razrushil? Pushkin!" *Gorod (812)*, no. 39 (192), December 11, 2012. https://gorod-812.ru/sovetskie-legendyi-kto-podzhigal-dvortsyi-pushkina-i-petergofa-v-voynu/.

Peri, Alexis. *The War Within: Diaries from the Siege of Leningrad.* Harvard, MA: Harvard University Press, 2017.

Petergof v Velikoi Otechestvennoi voine: 1941-1945. Vol. 2. Saint-Petersburg: GMZ "Petergof," 2019.

Petrov, Igor, and Ivan Tolstoi. "Na svete nravstvennom zagadka," *Radio Liberty/ Free Europe*, November 15, 2021. https://www.svoboda.org/a/na-svete-nravst-vennom-zagadka/31561053.html.

Platt, Jonathan Brooks. *Greetings, Pushkin! Stalinist Cultural Politics and the Russian National Bard.* Pittsburgh, NJ: University of Pittsburgh Press, 2016.

Qualls, Karl D. *Stalin's Niños: Educating Spanish Civil War Refugee Children in the Soviet Union, 1937-1951.* Toronto: University of Toronto Press, 2020.

Rutherford, Jeff. *Combat and Genocide on the Eastern Front: The German Infantry's War, 1941-1944.* Cambridge: Cambridge University Press, 2014.

Smith, Douglas. *Former People: The Final Days of the Russian Aristocracy*. New York: Picador, Farrar, Straus, and Giroux, 2013.

Sribnaia, A. V. "Organizatsiia deiatel'nosti sester miloserdiia v gody Pervoi mirovoi voiny," *Vestnik PSTGU, Seriia II*, no. 5 (60) (2014): 70–87.

———. *Sestry miloserdiia v gody Pervoi mirovoi voiny*. Moscow: Izd-vo TSTGU, 2017.

The Spanish Blue Division on the Eastern Front, 1941–1945: War, Occupation, Memory. Toronto: University of Toronto Press, 2022.

Tsypin, V. *Gorod Pushkin v gody voiny*. Saint-Petersburg: Genio Loci, 2019.

Velikanova, Olga. *Mass Political Culture under Stalinism: Popular Discussion of the Soviet Constitution of 1936*. Cham: Palgrave Macmillan, 2018.

Voronina, T. *Pomnit' po-nashemu: Sotsrealisticheskii istorizm i blokada Leningrada*. Moscow: Novoe Literaturnoe Obozrenie, 2018.

Yurchak, Alexei. *Everything Was Forever, until It Was No More: The Last Soviet Generation*. Princeton, NJ: Princeton University Press, 2006.

Zolotonosov, M. V. *Gadiushnik: Leningradskaia pisatel'skaia organizatssiia; izbrannye stenogrammu s kommentariiami; Iz istorii sovetskogo literaturnogo byta 1940–1960-kh godov*. Moscow: Novoe Literaturnoe Obozrenie, 2013.

Index